THE ULTIMATE JUGGLING BOOK

An Illustrated Guide to Tricks and Techniques

Written by
Richard Dingman

Illustrated by
Robert Frawley

COURAGE
BOOKS

AN IMPRINT OF RUNNING PRESS
PHILADELPHIA • LONDON

© 1996 by Running Press

Illustrations © 1996 by Robert Frawley

Printed in China

9   8   7   6   5   4   3   2   1

Digit on the right indicates the number
of this printing

Library of Congress Cataloging-in-Publication
Number 96-67157

ISBN 1-56138-773-8

Book cover and package design by Diane Miljat
Interior design by Stan Green
Edited by Elaine M. Bucher

Published by Courage Books, an imprint of
Running Press Book Publishers
125 South Twenty-Second Street
Philadelphia, Pennsylvania 19103-4399

Contents

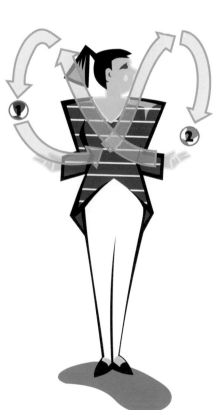

Introduction

First, let's clear some things up. Juggling is not something only a gifted few can learn. Almost anyone who can wonder at beauty, laugh at themselves, appreciate life, and enjoy dropping things will soon get the hang of the basics.

Learning to juggle does not mean that one day you will have to put on a red plastic nose and fake purple hair and juggle rubber chickens on street corners. Juggling is an ancient and respected art, with a history that can be traced back more than 4,000 years.

This Book Is About Juggling, But . . .

This book will introduce you to that art. You'll start by juggling one ball—you have to start somewhere. Then you'll move on to bigger and better things—juggling two balls, the basic three-ball cascade, juggling three clubs, how to eat an apple while you juggle. Finally, you'll learn advanced moves, like juggling four, five, or six balls, or passing clubs with both hands while standing on your head on a free-standing ladder. (That one may take a while.) For anyone willing to learn, here is a simple guide to keeping things up in the air.

So get ready—you're about to become a juggler.

The Wide World of Juggling

Most people know what juggling isn't. Juggling isn't mountain climbing, or poker, or meditation. But what about pistol spinning, baton twirling, hula hoops or hacky-sacks? If you think juggling is just throwing and catching three or more objects, get ready to expand your vision. Even among experts, juggling, like art and humor, falls into that category of things that won't be pinned down precisely, even though everyone claims to know what it is when they see it.

A controversy that occurred at an International Jugglers Association (IJA) numbers competition illustrates this point. The numbers event is one of several categories of competitions that the IJA sponsors. In the numbers competitions, individuals and teams vie to see who can juggle the most objects. Jugglers compete in various categories, each category utilizing a different common juggling object, such as a ball, ring, or club. Guidelines require a minimum number of throws and catches at each level to verify that competitors have successfully juggled that number of objects.

In 1979, a competitor confounded the judges by employing an obscure juggling technique called multiplexing to defeat his rivals. In multiplexing, objects are not thrown and caught one at a time, but in combinations of two or three at a time, enabling the juggler to keep more objects in the air with fewer throws and catches—and therefore fewer opportunities for error. Naturally, objections were made, much discussion ensued, and the multiplexer was eventually disqualified. Subsequently, multiplexing has been banned from numbers competitions in order to level the playing field.

But, despite the controversy over multiplexing in numbers competitions, most people would still consider it juggling. After all, people are certainly throwing and catching things—lots of things. It really looks a lot like juggling!

There are other varieties of the sport, however, that don't look very much like traditional juggling at all. Club swinging, for example, blurs the boundaries of juggling with gymnastics and object manipulation.

Club swinging refers to the manipulation of two clubs (the bowling-pin shaped objects that jugglers throw around), one in each hand, without letting go of either club. In the early 20th century, club swinging was an Olympic gymnastic event, having originated as a warm-up and exercise technique in many gymnasiums and athletic clubs across America. In 1948, however, it was dropped from the Olympic gymnastics program, along with the trampoline, the flying rings, and long tumbling runs.

Allan Jacobs, a professional juggler from New York City, was introduced to club swinging in the late 1970s by Phineas Indritz, who had been a member of the U.S. Olympic gymnastics team in 1936. Jacobs's subsequent juggling performance, incorporating a dynamic technical club swinging routine, won him the International Jugglers Association's Senior Competition in 1983. At the time, many grumbled over the fact that such a "nontraditional" juggling routine was allowed, but club swinging has since caught on among jugglers. Jacobs's club swinging workshops have been among the most popular workshops at recent IJA festivals.

So maybe juggling isn't necessarily always throwing and catching. And maybe you don't always have to juggle multiple objects. But you do need to incorporate at least two objects, right? Guess again.

Contact juggling obscures the boundaries between juggling, dance, and other movement performances. In contact juggling, as the name implies, the juggler remains in contact with the object. Not only are the elements of throwing and catching removed from the repertoire of the performer, but the number of objects employed is often strikingly limited. Instead, the juggled or manipulated object or objects are moved in continuous contact with the juggler's body—on, around, about, over, and under.

Contact juggling has become popular in the past decade, in part due to the beautiful, original, and often-copied work of Michael Moschen. Moschen began by juggling a crystal ball without ever grasping or closing his hands over the object. He moved his hand and body underneath the ball, which remained in one place, and created the illusion that the ball was acting independently of his body. Later, Moschen was able to create this same perceptual illusion in mesmerizing routines with sticks and rings.

Even more varieties of juggling exist within our own culture and in others around the world. Many of us are able to remember seeing juggling performers either in person or on television. During the 1950s and 1960s, television programs such as the *Ed Sullivan Show*, which highlighted many vaudeville performers, showcased jugglers rolling hoops around the stage and around their own bodies, spinning plates atop endless forests of pointed sticks, and balancing impossibly large, heavy, and unmanageable objects on their chins, noses, foreheads, and feet. Some also featured a clown-juggler who would tie himself in knots like a contortionist while taking off or putting on common articles of clothing.

Europeans, particularly the French, are more familiar with antipodism, a style of foot-juggling common in theater shows and circuses. The performer lies on his back with his legs up and manipulates, spins, rolls, tosses, and catches objects on the soles of his or her feet. When the

juggled object is another human being, this skill is called *risley*.

In Japan, a traditional juggling routine requires the performer to roll various objects around the rim of a delicate, inflated parasol. Great skill lies in rolling the objects, which may not even be round, as slowly as possible on the very edge of the parasol. Japanese performers also practice the art of *ken dama*. At its simplest, *ken dama* is a child's game involving the catching of a ball with a hole in it on a pointed stick held in the hand. The ball and the stick are connected by a short piece of string. In the hands of an expert, *ken dama* is a fascinating, rapid-fire routine with unexpected balances, tosses, and catches.

Chinese audiences are familiar with vase tossing, a difficult and dangerous form of juggling involving the tossing and catching (usually on the forehead) of huge, heavy ceramic vases. China is also home to the devil stick and diabolo. The devil stick routine consists of spinning, tossing, and catching a stick (known as the devil stick) by hitting it with two other sticks held in the hands. The devil stick itself is never touched. Experts manipulate a devil stick with each hand independently.

The diabolo is a cylindrical object that rolls along a string attached at each end to sticks held in the hands. By whipping the string from side to side, the diabolo spins very rapidly and can be rolled, tossed, and caught on the string. Accomplished performers can manipulate two or even three diabolos on one string simultaneously.

Each of these art forms, from contact juggling to French antipodism, borrows from or is related to (to lesser and greater degrees) traditional toss juggling. Therefore, despite the differences that separate them, their practitioners are all characterized as jugglers.

One would certainly see most if not all of the above-mentioned styles of juggling at an IJA festival. The festivals showcase both traditional styles—such as ball, club, ring, hat, and cigar box tossing—and lesser known varieties of the sport—including baton twirling, yo-yoing, flag and scarf tossing, kite flying, ribbon waving, revolver spinning, rope twirling, and whip cracking.

Quite obviously, juggling is not a sport that's easy to pin down. So, what is juggling? According to the dictionary, it's any manipulation of objects to produce a desired end. The vague nature of this definition allows juggling to incorporate a whole assortment of creative techniques and innovative ideas. The connotative definition of juggling changes with each new performance and routine. Clearly, if you can move something with your body in an interesting way, you can consider yourself part of the colorful and ancient tradition called juggling.

The History of Juggling

Nobody really knows how, when, or where juggling began. Long associated with magic and itinerant performers, jugglers were often considered outcasts. As a result, little historical data concerning the sport has been preserved.

The first depiction of juggling appears in Egyptian tomb paintings dating from 1900 B.C. Until approximately A.D. 500, depictions of jugglers were rare in the Western world, appearing mainly in tombs and literature from the Middle East. Around the year 1000, however, jugglers were mentioned more frequently, usually in association with traveling minstrels and cultlike religious groups of questionable morals and low social status. It wasn't until roughly 1500 that juggling became an accepted form of recreation in Europe.

It was in the 19th century, however, that juggling gained significant popularity. An infusion of Oriental performance art in the West helped to popularize juggling in European and American theaters. By the 20th century, most jugglers were able to find work in circuses and in vaudeville, where they were supported as part of a larger company of performers. In the latter half of the century, better props, information, inspiration, and more leisure time have contributed to another juggling revival. Jugglers are combining forces to push their art to inspired levels of difficulty and originality. The scope of interest, diversity, technical mastery, and popular acceptance of juggling throughout the world far exceeds previous standards, and there is little to suggest that this trend will not continue well into the future.

Getting Started

Choose Your Weapons

Let's begin. But where? Any place without distractions will work. (That goes for state of mind more than locale.) You must be able to concentrate. And the less furniture, the better.

First, you have to choose your props. For the very young or timid, light gauze-like scarves work great. Otherwise, most of you aspiring jugglers will appreciate the satisfying feel of rubber or silicone balls and fairly full beanbags. Whatever you choose, if you can hold just three of them in one hand, they're a good size.

First Things First

You could say there are three rules in juggling: relax, relax, and relax. Relax your muscles, relax your vision, relax your mind. Let's see how they work together.

Stand as if you were holding a tray of food on your outstretched palms. You should have your elbows at your sides and your forearms extended straight in front of you. Your hands should be slightly farther apart than your shoulders, and neither foot should be farther forward than the other. This is the basic position in which you will learn and execute the cascade, the fundamental juggling pattern.

Remember as you struggle that as long as you practice, you will improve. It's a universal law; you can't prevent it. Concentrate on what you are doing and you will learn even faster. And keep in mind that experts working on really hard stuff always improve more slowly than beginners, so have fun now—you won't be a beginner for long.

Step One: Juggling One Ball

Pick up one ball and hold it in your preferred, or starting, hand. Toss the ball up so that it peaks around the top of your head and falls into your other hand without your having to move that hand much. Now toss it back with the other hand, again making it peak around the top of your head. Make sure it lands back in the starting hand without your having to move much.

Do this for three to four minutes, or until it starts feeling easy and you hardly have to think

about it. Be sure to develop both hands equally so you won't have a weak side. Congratulations—you're already a third of the way toward being an actual juggler.

Extra Fun with One Ball

The goal of the first exercise is to develop accurate throws. If you can throw accurately, catching becomes much easier.

When you no longer have to move your catching hand, try some trick throws. Change the position of your throwing hand while keeping your catching hand in the same place.

For example, throw the ball from behind your back. Carry the ball behind your back with your throwing hand, then toss it straight up and over the opposite shoulder so that it lands easily in the catching hand.

Or make the toss from under your leg. Lift one leg (not both) with the knee high and bent, and carry the ball under the knee. Throw the ball up so that it lands in your catching hand.

Try bouncing the ball off the floor or wall, or roll it off your head. Vary the height and speed of your tosses. Juggle on your knees or while walking. All of this will keep you entertained and will prepare you for later exercises.

Step Two: Juggling Two Balls

After warming up with one ball, stand in the basic posture with one ball in each hand. Toss the ball from your starting hand to your other hand. Remember to throw to top-of-head height.

What happens? You end up with two balls in your alternate hand. The way to avoid ending up with two balls in your alternate hand is to empty it before the incoming ball arrives. Here's how it's done.

Let's call the ball in the starting hand Ball #1 and the ball in the other hand Ball #2. When Ball #1 is in the air just past its peak, toss Ball #2 underneath Ball #1. Your catching hand will now be empty and ready to catch Ball #1. In the end you will again hold one ball in each hand, but the balls will have changed hands.

Try it.

Did it happen? Probably not, unless you happen to be the Mozart of juggling. Most likely, both balls scattered and you have no idea what went wrong. But that's okay. In fact, watching well-controlled people completely lose it is one of the things that make teaching juggling so much fun.

What to do? Don't ask questions, try not to think too much, don't worry at all about catching, and try it again. Just do it a few times until you can observe and understand what's supposed to happen.

Now let's see what may be causing you trouble:

● Are all your throws reaching the same height, the height you reached when you did the one-ball exercise? If not, practice until they do.

● Are you moving your alternate hand from the basic position to throw under (not over) the incoming ball, and are you returning it to the

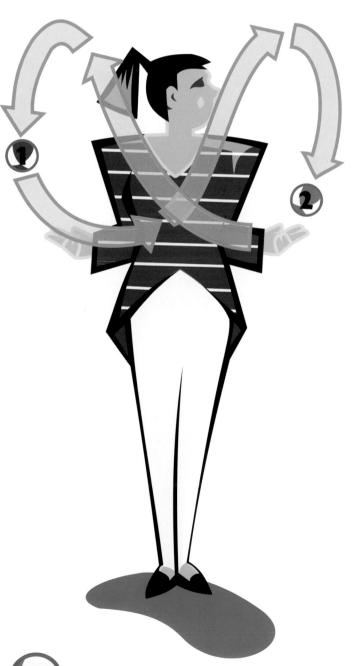

basic position to catch the incoming ball? You should be. If your alternate is moving properly it will make a small circle in the air.

● Do you jerk your hands upward prematurely to catch the balls? Relax and let them fall to you. It will give you more time to catch.

Once you think you've got it, pay attention to the rhythm of the juggle. What you should feel is this: "Throw, throw, catch, catch," equally timed, like four quarter-notes in a bar of 4/4 music.

Repeating that short mantra while you're juggling may help you keep your rhythm: "Throw,

throw, catch, catch. Throw, throw, catch, catch." And so on.

Don't be discouraged when you drop the balls. Take a deep breath, shake out the tension, and give it another try. If you can get feedback from another juggler or from a friend who can watch and critique you, get some. It could save you from developing bad habits. Even a non-juggler can tell if your throws are not all at the same height or not rhythmically even.

Keep practicing the two-ball juggle, or exchange, until you've got it down cold. This is the fundamental skill for almost every other juggling pattern—its importance cannot be overemphasized.

And besides, now you're two thirds of the way there.

Extra Fun with Two Balls

Now that you've mastered the exchange, you're almost ready to add that third ball. But here's some other fun stuff you can try first. (Come back to this section later if you're all worked up about juggling that third ball.)

The trick throws you practiced earlier can be practiced here, this time with two balls. Execute your trick throw first—over your shoulder, off your elbow, under your leg, whatever—then finish the exchange with a normal toss. Be sure you are able to maintain the rhythm.

If you want a more advanced exercise, try to substitute the trick throw for the *second* exchange toss, or for both throws. This isn't easy, and it requires close attention to rhythm and accuracy.

You may find that trick throws you thought you had down cold are difficult to do when they become part of a larger pattern. This is normal, and it may cause frustration.

But you must learn the basics thoroughly—not just with your brain, which learns and forgets quickly, but with your muscles as well. Muscles learn more slowly, and only by frequent repetition.

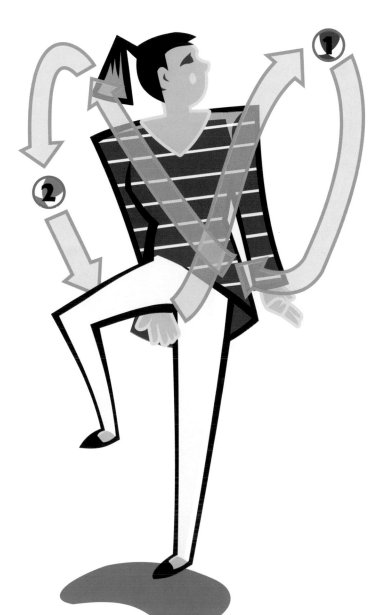

Step Three: Juggling Two in One Hand

To do this one-handed juggle, hold two balls in one hand. Pick your dominant hand to learn with first. As soon as you begin to feel comfortable with this move, practice it with your alternate hand as well.

Hold one ball (hereafter Ball #1) with your index finger, middle finger and thumb so that it does not touch your palm. Toss it straight up in the air. This time, however, it should peak one or

two feet *above* your head. The extra height will give you more time.

Catch this throw and repeat it several times. Notice that you tend to throw from out on the tips of your fingers and catch farther back toward the palm.

Once you've got that, hold the other ball (hereafter Ball #2) in the middle of your palm, securely cradled between your ring finger, pinkie,

Throw Ball #1 into the air. When it leaves your hand, roll Ball #2 onto the tips of your fingers. Then, gently toss Ball #2 into the air. Be sure to toss it slightly to the side of Ball #1—you don't want them to collide in midair! Your hand is now empty to catch Ball #1.

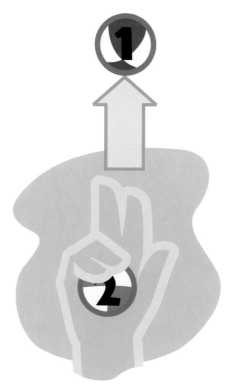

and the meaty part of your thumb. Ball #1 is in the throwing position. The catching position is in the middle of your hand, closer to where Ball #2 is. You'll feel it naturally when you get going.

With both balls in position, throw Ball #1. When it leaves your hand, roll Ball #2 into Ball #1's empty spot. Toss it up to the same height, but slightly to one side. Now your hand is empty and ready to catch Ball #1 as it falls back to hand level.

To finish, catch Ball #1 in the catching part of the hand and then catch Ball #2 in the throwing part of the hand. Eureka! Practice each hand separately.

The big question with this move is usually "How do I avoid collision?" One way is to throw on the inside and to catch on the outside. This is what most people do when they learn to juggle two balls in one hand.

However, circling the balls in the opposite direction is fine too. Tossing the balls straight up and down side by side is also okay. Try all the different methods with each hand and decide which you like best.

Step Four: Juggling Three Balls

Still here? Congratulations, you've learned a lot already, almost all the basics! If you've learned them well, you won't have any trouble with this next step—the simple but impressive leap to juggling three balls.

Start by warming up, as always. Some gentle aerobics followed by gentle stretches of your choice help to prevent injuries. Go through all the basics to thoroughly warm up your juggling muscles.

Now stand with two balls in your dominant hand and one ball in the other. We'll call the ball between the thumb and the first two fingers of the starting hand Ball #1 and the ball in the palm of that same hand Ball #3. The ball in the other hand is Ball #2.

Toss Ball #1 from the starting hand to the alternate hand and back again, making sure that it peaks at about head height. Do this a few times until you are used to throwing a ball from a hand with two balls. When you feel ready for the next step, stop with two balls in your starting hand and one in the other.

Now begin the exchange. Toss Ball #1 from your starting hand to your alternate hand, then Ball #2 to the starting hand. Catch Ball #1 in the alternate hand.

If we freeze the situation at this instant, we find Ball #3 in your starting hand, Ball #1 in your alternate hand, and Ball #2 in the air, traveling toward your starting hand. Now unfreeze.

When Ball #2 passes its peak and begins to fall toward your starting hand, empty that hand

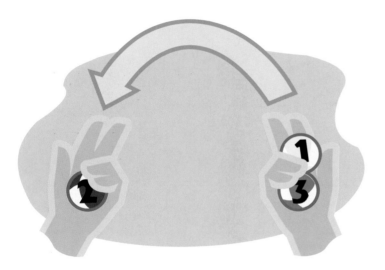

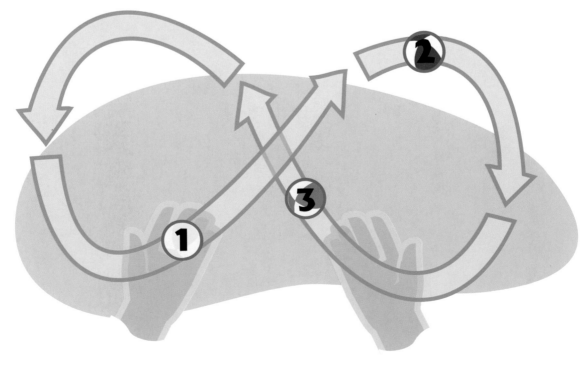

by tossing Ball #3 underneath Ball #2. Catch Ball #2 in your starting hand.

Freezing the moment again, we now see one ball in each hand and Ball #3 in the air, on its way to your alternate hand. Now unfreeze again.

Toss Ball #1 back to the starting hand and catch Ball #3 as it drops. As Ball #1 peaks, toss Ball #2 from your starting hand, then catch Ball #1, toss Ball #3 again, and so on, and so on, and so on.

With this pattern there will always be a ball in each hand and a third in the air, except at the moment of exchange.

Congratulations! You did it! But if you didn't, keep on trying until you do. If you've gotten this far, you know it's just a matter of time and patience.

The description is really more complicated than the actual event. Once you understand the exchanges and can link them together, one immediately following the other, then you understand how to juggle three balls.

Experts speed up the process by lowering the heights of the tosses. This gives the appearance of a unified event rather than the sequence of awkwardly linked stages that every beginner's juggle resembles.

Troubleshooting

Here are some things to remember if you're having problems:

Keep your hands at tray-holding height and make sure every single one of your throws peaks at the same height, about the top of your head. If you find yourself beginning to walk forward because your throws lead you that way, take heart, you are not the first. Your affliction is called "beginner's walk," and it's easily cured by practicing in front of a bed or a solid wall. You will soon be cured—or in a lot of pain.

Don't spend a lot of time struggling to understand the instructions if the juggle doesn't come quickly. Just throw the balls around as best you can after reading the directions. If you have a problem, keep trying until you get a sense of

where you're messing up. Then consult this book again for help. Your mind will make this more complicated than it really is, and that can drain your motivation.

Remember, you're more likely to learn juggling by doing than by studying. It's not like school—you won't avoid the normal beginner's mistakes by studying hard the night before.

Just do it. At some point it will all click, and then it's all smiles.

Advanced Juggling Fun

Unless you've skipped a section, you are now juggling three balls.

You're also probably counting how many catches you can make before dropping a ball. This is big fun. But when you can keep three balls airborne for more than a hundred catches, you'll want more juggling excitement.

Varying the height and speed of your tosses is much more satisfying with a three-ball pattern. As you lower your tosses the pattern tightens up and looks more impressive.

Just for fun, see how high or low, fast or slow, wide or narrow you can juggle. Juggle while you're walking, turning, or even jogging. (Joggling—juggling while jogging—is a popular sport. There are even joggling record-holders who run the normal track and cross-country distances while juggling!)

More Advanced Fun: The Reverse Cascade

While juggling your three-ball pattern, notice the path that one ball travels. This is easy to see if you use one differently colored ball in your juggle. If you run the pattern backward, you'll learn another essential juggling move—the reverse cascade.

To accomplish the reverse cascade, first practice with one ball in each hand, as you did when you juggled two balls. Remember that when you juggled two balls you always threw the second ball *under* the incoming ball. For the reverse cascade, try throwing the second ball *over* the incoming ball. It will feel awkward at first. Practice it with both hands for five minutes.

Next, juggle three balls regularly and concentrate on the way all of your throws come under the incoming balls. This is the normal cascade pattern.

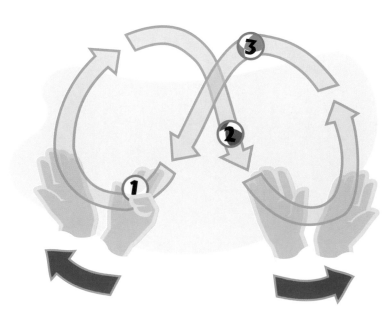

Now get ready to start the reverse cascade. Toss one of your throws *over* one of the incoming balls instead of under it. Then go back to your cascade.

When you can, increase the frequency of these over-the-ball tosses until every throw you make is a reverse cascade throw.

Even More Advanced Fun: Trick Throws, the Shower, and Others

Before you hit the streets with an empty hat and high hopes, let's add some more tricks to your repertoire. Use the trick throws you perfected earlier: under your leg, behind your back, rolling off your head, bouncing off the floor—anything you want. Rapid sequencing of several basic tricks can create beautiful and complex-looking moves, letting you run wild with your artistic impulses. And don't forget trying to alternate between your cascade and juggling two balls in one hand.

Though the cascade (and the reverse cascade) is the fundamental three-ball juggling pattern, it isn't the only one. One of the others you can try is the shower.

To begin the shower, start in cascade position, with two balls in one hand and one in the other. With the shower, however, you'll throw the balls in a different order, so we'll number them differently. Call the ball on the fingers of the starting hand Ball #1, the ball in the palm of the starting hand Ball #2, and the ball in the other hand Ball #3.

First, throw Ball #1 toward your alternate hand. Pick a height about a foot or two higher than your cascade height—the shower is a faster pattern. Before Ball #1 passes its peak, toss Ball #2 in exactly the same path as Ball #1. Immediately after releasing Ball #2, toss Ball #3 to your starting hand. (This toss, called a shower throw, is thrown to the starting hand in the shortest, most direct line possible. With a little practice you will be able to do this without even looking at your hands.)

Now your alternate hand is empty and able to catch Ball #1. Continue the pattern in this way, with the balls moving in one large circle rather than in the "lazy eight" pattern of the cascade.

Notice that the shower and the cascade have

different rhythms. You can hear the difference as the balls hit your hands. The cascade has a very regular beat (catch, catch, catch, catch), while the shower has a kind of 3/4 rhythm (catch, catch, pause, catch, catch, pause).

Almost all the patterns you can do by throwing balls up in the air you can also do by throwing them down to the floor and catching them as they bounce back. Bounce juggling will work well anywhere you have a flat, hard floor.

Lightly toss the balls up and let them fall at their own speed to the floor. Catch them with your other hand as they come up, either before or after they peak. This is a very slow, relaxed way to do a three-ball cascade off the floor.

A faster way is called the forced bounce, in which you throw the balls directly at the floor instead of softly lobbing them into the air. This makes for a much faster pattern and takes a little more practice. Either bounce juggle can be incorporated into any juggling routine, so experiment!

If you've mastered two balls in one hand, why not try three? To people who can't juggle three balls in two hands, this will look very impressive. You begin with a three-ball cascade if holding and releasing three balls with one hand is too difficult. (This may depend as much upon your hand size as your abilities.) The whole trick lies in maintaining an accurate nonintersecting pattern—either a cascade, independent columns, or a circle—keeping all your throws the same height, and keeping a regular, rapid rhythm.

If your wrists and arms are getting tired, try juggling with your feet! Kick-ups, popularized by Michael Kass, use the feet and the hands both. In this variation, balls or beanbags are caught on the toes and lifted back up into your juggling pattern. Clubs can also be used (although they are more difficult to manipulate). Caught on the top of the foot—fat end out and forward, or fat end in and back—the clubs are flipped back up to the hand without ever touching the floor.

The best tricks of all, though, will be the ones you discover on your own. Experiment with what you've learned and be inventive! Not only will your personal tricks astound your audience, but they will be tremendously satisfying for you.

Still More Advanced Fun: Eating an Apple

If you've ever watched professional jugglers perform, either on the streets or on television, you've probably seen one of them eat an apple while juggling. It's pretty impressive, but you can do it too. Here's how.

First, you need to be able to juggle three balls without having to watch your hands much—except with peripheral vision.

Next, you need to learn a new catch.

Start with the cascade. Just before a toss from your alternate hand peaks, move your starting

hand out of position to catch it higher than you normally would. Slap your hand upward to grab the incoming ball in the air, and continue to carry it up slightly. Then lower your hand to its normal position in time to throw and maintain the cascade pattern. When you can do this smoothly, you'll begin your upward motion even before the starting hand unloads the previous ball. Don't be deterred by drops and balls flying every which way. Keep practicing—you'll get it.

When you do, try it with your weak hand as well. Then practice slowly raising the slap-caught ball higher and higher until it is at your mouth. You may find it helpful to slow your cascade by raising the heights of your throws.

The rest comes easily. Substitute an apple for the ball you will catch and bring toward your mouth, and start chomping. You can take extra-long bites by briefly juggling two balls in your other hand.

If you really want to make an impression, be creative with your fruits and vegetables. Eat an onion or a big juicy tomato. Try extremely high tosses with peaches—throw them ten feet into the air and catch them in your mouth.

Just make sure they're very, very ripe.

Step Five: Juggling More Than Three Balls

If you've gotten this far and followed each exercise, you're a three-ball juggler. Terrific! Many of the best-known juggling performances consist of skill, imagination, and just three balls. But sit tight—you're about to go where very few have gone before.

There are many jugglers who aren't content to stop at three balls. These brave souls wonder what it's like to juggle four balls, or five balls, or six balls, or even more.

"Difficult" is what it's like. The more objects you juggle, the harder it gets, and the longer it takes to get there. But for those of you with the courage to try, here's how you do it.

First, try learning odd numbers. The cascade is usually the easiest pattern for juggling any odd number—three, five, seven, or more.

To juggle five balls you need to be able to:

1. Hold three balls in one hand and still toss one ball from that hand accurately. (Ball #1 is held between the thumb and index finger, Ball #2 is held on top of the middle finger and pinched between the index and ring fingers, and Ball #3 is held against the rear of the palm by the tips of the ring and pinkie fingers. The beginning throws usually occur with the starting hand turned so that the thumb is on top, palm inward, if this feels natural.)

2. Raise your throw heights at least two feet to give yourself more time.

3. Release the second ball from your alternate hand *before* Ball #1 peaks.

4. Concentrate on maintaining a quick, even rhythm.

5. Dedicate six months, minimum.

Juggling even numbers is a different matter, since you can't do a cascade with an even number of objects. Try it and you'll see why.

To juggle four balls, some enthusiasts like to

juggle two balls in one hand and two balls in the other. If you want to do it this way, you can use a couple of different patterns.

Throw the four balls straight up and down in columns or in two separate circles, one clockwise and the other counter-clockwise. You can even throw balls in both hands at the same time (in sync), or alternately (out of sync).

Other four-ball jugglers use the half-cascade pattern. Hold two balls in each hand and throw, simultaneously, one ball from each hand over to the other hand. You can avoid collisions by having one hand deliver cascade throws (under the ball), and the other deliver reverse cascade throws (over the ball).

The hand throwing reverse cascade tosses should throw a split-second *before* the other hand. The technique is similar for juggling six or eight balls, but you'll need a lot of free time.

Any number of balls can also be juggled in the shower pattern. However, since this pattern is inherently faster than the cascade, it's even tougher to apply it to the higher numbers.

The Greatest Numbers Juggler: ENRICO RASTELLI

Enrico Rastelli (1897–1931), one of the world's most famous jugglers and arguably the greatest ever, was born in Bergamo, Italy. From an early age he was trained by his father to be a circus performer, practicing religiously for several hours every day. Before he was twenty, Rastelli was already internationally famous.

Rastelli was the first juggler to perform the now-popular routine in which juggling props are thrown into the audience and caught on a stick held in the juggler's mouth as they are tossed back to him. Many of his acts have been copied, and still are, but many were far too challenging for others to perform. Rastelli, for example, could balance a total of twelve balls on his body, many atop sticks. He could also juggle ten balls, a feat that has yet to be matched by any other juggler.

23

Step Six: Passing with a Friend

Passing is a type of juggling in which two or more jugglers throw lots of stuff at each other in what looks like total chaos—except that nothing drops (hopefully). It's pretty advanced, but if you and a friend are feeling confident, here's how it works.

What follows is a developmental series of elementary passing exercises. Find a partner who juggles about as well as you do and practice the exercises more or less in the order they are presented. In general, they are organized so that each exercise depends upon skills learned in previous exercises, but some amount of skipping around is possible.

It isn't strictly necessary, for example, to juggle three objects before you try juggling

2p1c (read as two people with 1 club) patterns and 2p2c (two people with two clubs) patterns. But by the time you reach 2p3c, you should be comfortable cascading the three objects you are passing. If not, your uncertainty will trip you up. Any three objects can be used, but I'll assume you are using clubs, the most irregular, difficult, and interesting of the traditional passing objects.

Clubs (don't call them pins if you want people to think you're a juggler!) are those bowling pin–shaped objects jugglers throw around. In the old days (roughly until World War II), clubs were made by the performer himself out of a wide variety of materials, mostly solid wood or wood strips. Back then, learning to juggle with clubs was often quite painful! Today, juggling

clubs have become fairly standardized. They are mostly made out of lightweight, sturdy plastics and come in a variety of colors. If you don't have a set of clubs, don't despair. Clubs are easy to obtain through the mail from several manufacturers in the United States and at select magic shops.

How to Make Sense of It All

Throughout this section you'll be introduced to some abbreviations that are used to discuss juggling throughout the rest of this book. These abbreviations are standard and are used by many juggling professionals. Ignore them at your peril.

When you watch your own 3c (read as three club) cascade, you'll notice that every club that lands in your left hand is thrown there from your right hand. Likewise, every club caught by your right hand is thrown by your left hand. Each

hand is responsible for getting its clubs in a position where the other hand can catch them. This may sound obvious, but it is the essential piece of information from which virtually all passing technique is logically derived.

In the cascade, throwing a club to someone else with your right hand removes a club from your juggle that would have otherwise landed in your left hand. Your passing partner is now responsible for filling that gap. He or she must make sure that the passed club is in the proper position at the proper time to be caught by your left hand.

As far as basic passing theory goes, that's all there is to it. No matter what you juggle—balls, rings, hats, or cats—the theory is the same. However, there are technical considerations that can make passing easier and conventions adopted by nearly all passers that will help you avoid confusion.

The Conventions

1. Timing—Proper timing is essential. Waiting for a late throw to arrive or rushing to empty your hand quickly because a pass has arrived too soon is terribly frustrating. Remember, your juggling partner expects you to place a club near his empty hand when *he* needs it!

2. Positioning—Your partner also expects that your pass will be in the proper position and therefore easy to catch. The ideal spot for a juggler to grab an incoming pass varies slightly from person to person, but the general rule is that the handle of the club should be approximately biceps height, slightly outside the arm (enough so that if the catcher did nothing, the club would pass harmlessly by), and about six inches in front of the body. This is the preferred position for vertically caught clubs, but some trick throws will require clubs to be caught in different positions.

3. Orientation—Orientation refers to the angle of the club in the air when caught. For most throws, the standard orientation is vertical, handle down. The club is caught with the hand open, palm forward, fingers pointing out (away from the center of the body), and thumb pointing in.

There are many other possible orientations, and some you will discover by accident. That's fine—feel free to experiment. Just be sure you can deliver the club in the right position and orientation and at the proper time. Your consistency will make you a popular passing partner.

4. Speed—Whether you pass quickly or slowly is up to you and your partner, but a certain confident zip in a pass will help it slap into your catching hand with a satisfyingly solid feel that you will soon come to enjoy and expect.

5. Stance—When passing, stand with feet even. While you might prefer advancing the left foot when passing with the right hand and vice versa, you will eventually have to abandon the practice when you graduate to passing with both hands, or you will be constantly shuffling your feet back and forth.

6. Throwing—Just as you throw from the inside and catch on the outside of a cascade pattern, you will also throw from the inside when passing to another person. In other words, the hand that releases a pass will then catch a self-throw on the outside of the cascade pattern (farther away from the body). This holds for the majority of passes. The movement may feel awkward at first, but it will help to avoid congested patterns by forcing you to keep your juggle spacious.

How much wrist versus arm you should use to spin your pass is very idiosyncratic. You will find your own form. Keep in mind that the more wrist you use, the faster and snappier your pattern will be. The more arm you use, the slower and more relaxed the pattern. Be versatile—different patterns suggest different techniques.

7. Attention—In the beginning, you've got about all you can handle keeping your cascade going while you launch a club now and then in the general direction of your partner. The beginner's eyes are glued to the clubs immediately in front of her, only briefly straying to catch glimpses of her partner in order to aim her throws.

As you become more confident, you will be able to view more of the pattern and pay more attention to what's happening around you. Eventually, you will watch your own cascade only peripherally. You'll look over your cascade to your partner, and by viewing the complete pattern with its continual variations you'll be able to adjust spontaneously to changes. Besides that, you'll get to enjoy what's going on.

8. Dropping—Don't forget to make sure that everyone has stopped passing before you look away to find fallen clubs. After one or two clubs have hit you in the head, you'll remember.

Juggling with Clubs

Before you start juggling clubs with your partner, let's go over the basics of juggling clubs by yourself. While juggling with clubs is almost exactly the same as juggling with balls, there is one important difference. Balls are "all handle" and can be caught anywhere. Clubs need to be spun in discrete, precise, full circles. You need to learn to flip the club exactly one complete turn. It's not that hard, but here are some helpful hints.

Don't hold the club at the very end of the handle. Choke up three or four inches so that your index finger is just about under the balance point of the club.

Next, let your index finger flip the club by pushing up at the balance point while your thumb presses down on the end of the handle. This way you won't need a lot of arm motion to throw the club from one hand to the other. Keep your elbows near your sides and your forearms parallel with the floor.

As you release the toss, angle the fat end of the club toward your catching hand. This will make the club much easier to catch.

Find a height and speed that is relaxed and natural. There is no need to whack yourself in the face or collarbone by tossing wild, hard throws. Once you get used to juggling with clubs you'll be able to lower the throws and speed up the spins. After you feel comfortable with single spins, try doubles. Don't spin the clubs much faster, just loft them a little higher—about three feet over your head.

To juggle two clubs in one hand you need only learn how to hold the two clubs so that you can release them accurately. Put one club (hereafter Club #2) across your palm, with the fat end sticking out between your thumb and index finger.

Place the other club (hereafter Club #1) across Club #2, with your index finger directly underneath the balance point of the club and the handle in your palm.

While Club #2 is held securely, the thumb and fingertips guide the first throw. Double spins are easiest to throw.

It just takes you-know-what—practice!

When you begin to juggle clubs, you may want to practice outdoors or in a large, open room. Clubs that go astray can cause quite a bit of damage in a crowded room! Always try to juggle on a soft, absorbent surface like a lawn or a carpet. This will protect your clubs from excess damage when you drop them—and you will drop them.

Step Seven: Passing Just One Club

Unless otherwise noted, the patterns discussed will be described in the most common configuration, two people face-to-face. All the patterns we will work with, however, are adaptable to many configurations (face-to-back, back-to-back, side-by-side, one person standing on the other's shoulders, etc.) with little or no modification.

You and your partner should face each other, about eight to twelve feet apart, with one club between you. Hold on a moment, don't be in any hurry to get anywhere. This isn't just a beginner's exercise, a novice's drudgery never to be encountered again after the required hours are put in. This 2p1c (read as two people with one club) position is an essential tool, a device that most jugglers return to even after becoming proficient at basic club passing. Any new, unfamiliar pass of sufficient difficulty will require the two jugglers to abandon all but one club to concentrate on the technique necessary for the new throw.

Right now all throws are sufficiently difficult for you to require full concentration. But no matter how many years you might juggle, there will always be sufficiently difficult throws.

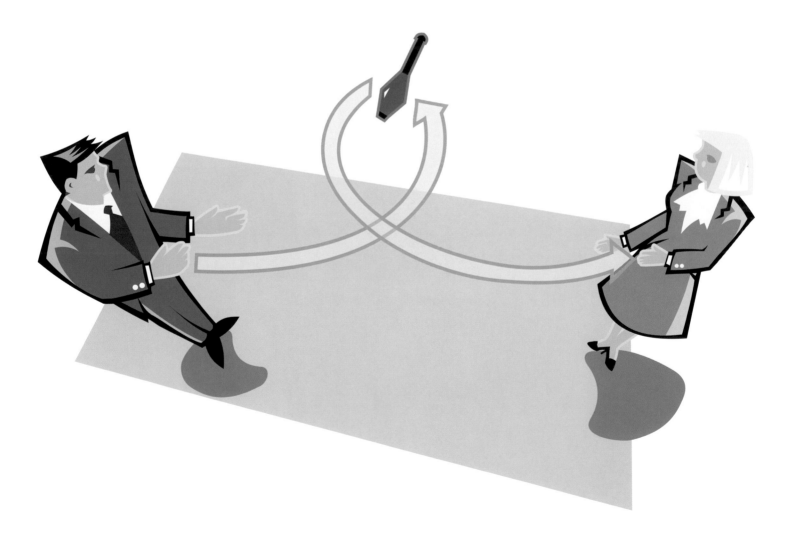

One Around

Enough words—let's start throwing some clubs.

Juggler A begins with one club in his right hand. His partner (hereafter Juggler B) has no clubs. Holding the club by the handle (not by the knob, but choked up about four inches), Juggler A's right hand swings down alongside the right leg and then forward again directly toward Juggler B's left hand, releasing the club with just enough spin to cause one revolution.

Actually, the club completes slightly more than one revolution (about $1^{1}/_{4}$) by the time it is caught. This is the standard pass, known as a single.

Make sure that the passing hand holds the club vertically. While you can angle the club toward your partner, you must not tilt the club to the right or to the left while it is swung and released. If the club is not released vertically it won't arrive in your partner's hand vertically.

Remember, the pass should be thrown to a spot a couple inches outside the catcher's arm, enough so that if the catcher did nothing, the club would pass harmlessly by and not whack him or her in the arm, neck, or head. Please reread this paragraph.

You don't want your single pass to be too slow and bloopy, though this may be your initial tendency. Overly tentative passes take extra effort to grab and will destroy the rhythm of your juggling. Your pass, however, should not be spun so quickly that the catcher can't "read" it (i.e., can't easily judge the rate of rotation and determine when and where to place his or her left hand to snag the handle on its way by).

Extremely fast passes are often out of control and a menace to all jugglers' inherent good looks. Be aware and monitor your own throws.

After Juggler B catches the club in her left hand, she flips it (with one rotation) to her right hand, just like in a three-club cascade. This is called a self-throw.

Juggler B proceeds to pass the club across to Juggler A's left hand. This right-handed pass from Juggler B to Juggler A is done in exactly the same way as the earlier pass from Juggler A to B. Juggler A catches the club in his left hand, self-throws a single to his right hand, and passes again to Juggler B's left hand. The pattern then repeats itself. Practice until you can maintain a steady rhythm of pass, self-throw, pass, self-throw.

Although one around is the easiest possible two-person pattern, it contains the seeds from which all other patterns will grow. You need to practice the pattern until you feel so comfortable that you can carry on a meaningful conversation while you juggle and even walk together in any direction—maintaining the same distance between you or intentionally increasing or decreasing that distance.

One Club, Right Hands (1c, RHs)

This is a variation on the previous pattern. In the one around pattern, all the passes (not self-throws; generally the term pass refers to an object thrown to another person, not to oneself) are parallel passes. A parallel pass is one that does not cross an imaginary line between one juggler's heart and his or her partner's heart.

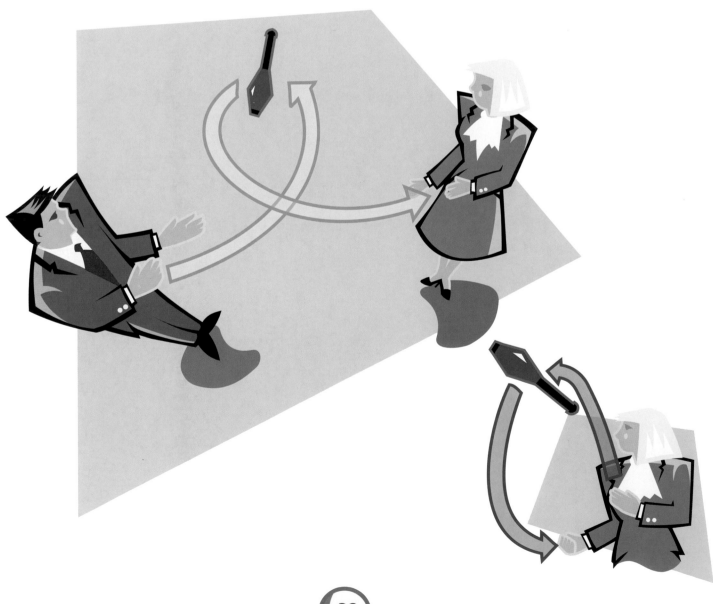

A cross pass is one that does.

In this new pattern (1c, RHs), both Juggler A and Juggler B throw cross passes; that is, Juggler A's right hand throws to Juggler B's right hand and vice versa. No left hands are used at all, so there are no self-throws.

Here, the right hands are beginning to learn to catch as well as to throw. For variety, mix the last two patterns. One of you can juggle one around while the other juggles 1c, RHs. Then switch.

One Around Doubles

This is the same as one around except that all the passes are doubles instead of singles. A double is a pass that rotates twice before it is caught. For the pass to have time to rotate twice, it must be thrown higher. The double shouldn't turn much faster than the single—it should just stay in the air longer.

Before you try this pattern, you should practice self-doubles alone with one club. Throw doubles from hand to hand until you begin to feel comfortable. You want to become so sensitive to the feel of the proper release that you don't have to watch the club to know it has been spun correctly.

Don't let your hands rise much higher than your waist, and keep them shoulder width apart.

Now try doubles with your partner.

Remember, if you spin the club too fast it's hard to know when to stick your mitt into the air to catch the handle. Be relaxed when you throw the club and keep the doubles rotating at the same speed as the singles.

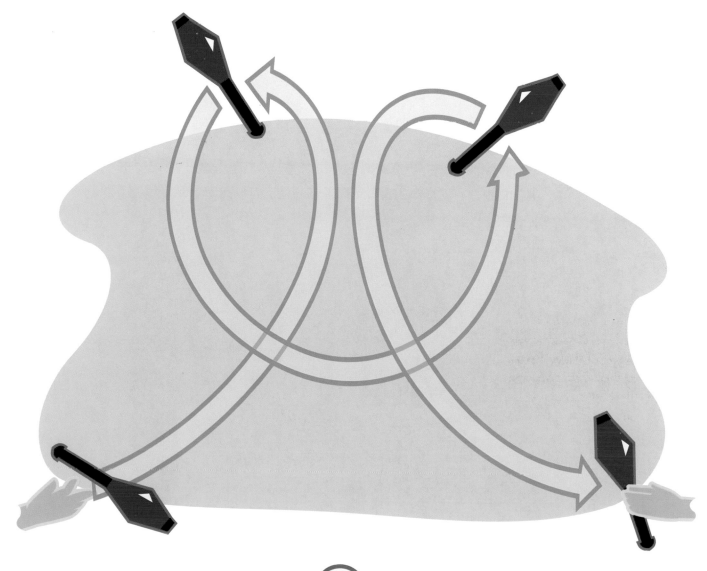

One Club, Right Hands, Doubles

This is a combination of the two previous exercises and is pretty self-explanatory. Concentrate on making your passes land precisely where and how you want them to land. Ideally, you should be able to drop your pass, single or double, exactly into your partner's hand so that he or she doesn't have to move an inch to catch an incoming club. When you think you're that good, prove it. Catch the passes with your eyes closed.

But please, throw them with your eyes open.

One Around, Drop-Ups, and Drop-Backs

This final 2p1c (two people with one club) pattern requires a new configuration, namely front-to-back. Juggler A should stand approximately four or five feet behind Juggler B, facing his partner's back. In this configuration, the throws that Juggler A makes to Juggler B are called drop-ups and the throws that Juggler B makes to Juggler A are called drop-backs.

To begin, all passes should be right-handed parallel passes. Let's consider the drop-ups first. There are two new things to learn with these passes.

First, they are not caught in the same way you've been catching passes up to now. Drop-ups and drop-backs are caught in almost exactly the same orientation as a self-thrown club (i.e., horizontally, handle toward you). Your catching hand should be open, palm up.

Second, when catching a drop-up Juggler B can't see it approaching until it is almost ready to be caught. Juggler B doesn't have much time to read incoming drop-ups, so they need to be especially well thrown. They need to be fairly high, relaxed passes to be optimally catchable. In addition, Juggler B should look up and slightly back to see the club as early as possible.

These passes are tricky and take a bit of practice. Helmets are a good idea for your first few attempts. But keep trying! Drop-ups and drop-backs will open up a tremendous number of passing possibilities.

Drop-backs are easier to get the knack of than drop-ups, at least for the catcher, since the receiver can see almost the entire trajectory and has plenty of time to read and prepare for the incoming club.

As with drop-ups, drop-backs are also doubles and are also caught in the same orientation as a self-thrown club. They are thrown by raising the club in the throwing hand and releasing it so that it arcs straight back and turns twice (technically, $1\frac{3}{4}$ turns) before being caught. Getting the

appropriate amount of spin is not easy, and the common tendency is to overturn the club. Very little wrist is needed at the moment of release, since the action of raising the club has already started it turning. Don't despair—you will eventually develop a feel for it.

Now try a drop-up and a drop-back. The catcher should give his or her partner feedback after every drop-back. Don't turn around to see how each of your drop-backs looks. Trust your partner's comments and concentrate on developing a feel for the throw. Don't forget to take a turn at each role.

Let's try one more variation before we move on. Stand back-to-back, almost touching, and throw drop-backs simultaneously. The throws are made nearly straight up over your passing hand's shoulder and caught with the hand upraised, palm open toward the sky. The club is caught slightly above your shoulder, horizontally, with the handle pointing forward. Doubles are easiest.

Left-Handed Passing

Every pass so far has been thrown by your right hand. That's pretty limiting, so let's get the left hand throwing too.

First, try one around with your left hand. This may be extremely difficult, but the sooner you become ambidextrous the better. It's not only tricky to learn how to throw with your left-hand, but it's also a bit awkward training your right hand to catch. (We've already had a little practice with that in 1c, RHs.)

Then work your left-handed way through:

1. 1c, LHs.
2. One around, LH, doubles.
3. 1c, LHs, doubles.
4. One around, drop-ups and drop-backs.

This is altogether quite a lot to work on, and we are still using only one club! Make sure you're feeling familiar, if not comfortable, with what we've learned so far before you head on to the next chapter. Your burdens are about to double.

Step Eight: Passing with Two Clubs

Two Around

A second club can be added to one around in such a way that both jugglers are always doing exactly the same thing at exactly the same time.

Both jugglers stand face-to-face with one club in their right hand. Each simultaneously passes a single to his partner's left hand and then self-throws to his own right hand. This pattern is then repeated.

Don't forget to practice the left-handed version as well. In fact, you might want to focus more on the left hand than on the right if your left hand is significantly weaker.

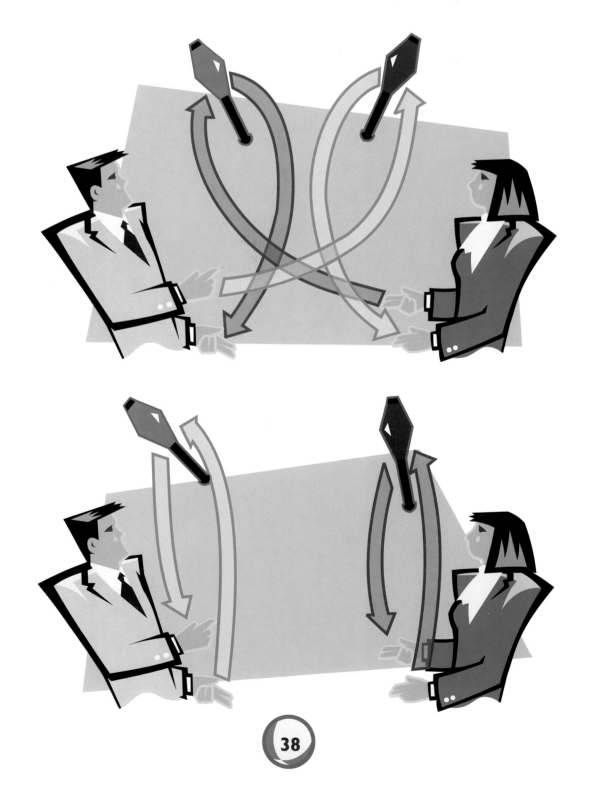

Two Around Doubles

This pattern is the same as the previous pattern with double-spun passes. (Self-throws can be singles or doubles, as you wish.) Work with your left hand too.

Once you are relaxed and can juggle two around doubles with some confidence, begin to notice the relative heights and rates of spin of the simultaneously thrown doubles. Both you and your partner can gain valuable experience by varying your own throws to match each other's.

Two Around, Drop-Ups and Drop-Backs

Using the front-to-back configuration, throw your drop-ups and drop-backs simultaneously. This is excellent practice and training for fuller patterns—patterns using at least three clubs per person.

HELPFUL HINT: Keep your passes parallel at the beginning. With parallel passes, one juggler will be passing with her right hand while the other will be passing with his left hand. Take turns at each role, and remember to switch positions so you have a chance to try all four variations.

Two Adjacent Around

This is one around with a second club added in such a way that both jugglers are never doing the same thing at the same time.

Facing one another, Juggler A has one club in each hand and Juggler B has no clubs. Juggler A begins by self-tossing the club from his left hand to his right hand. When the club is nearly at its peak, Juggler A empties his right hand by passing a club across to Juggler B's left hand. Juggler A then catches the club in his right hand and passes that club to Juggler B's left hand. Now Juggler A has no clubs.

Juggler B catches the first club in her left hand. When the second club is on its way to her left hand (somewhat before the middle of the trajectory), Juggler B begins to empty her left hand by self-passing the club from her left hand to her right. Juggler B catches the incoming club in her left hand and then catches the self-pass in her right hand. Now Juggler B is

in the same position Juggler A was when we began.

The most important aspect of this exercise is not how you manage to throw and catch the clubs—that proficiency will come in time. It is more important (lest you develop some bad habits that will haunt you in the future) that you are able to maintain an alternating rhythm with your hands. You should always throw one hand after the other, alternately, as long as there are clubs in your hands to be thrown.

This is quite difficult to explain in words and not easy for beginners to observe since two clubs in a passing pattern are not enough to force both hands to move alternately at every moment. This will become clearer as we increase the number of clubs in the pattern. It's advisable for you, if possible, to find a better juggler who will demonstrate and critique this exercise for you and who can correct your mistakes.

Step Nine: Passing with Three Clubs

Three Around

By now the how-ever-many around patterns are getting to be old hat. Not surprisingly, three around is also built on the one around pattern. But it's not just more of the same old stuff. The addition of the third club forces us to master the essential and fundamental aspect of passing—rhythm.

Juggler A begins juggling three clubs in a cascade, while his partner is empty-handed. When Juggler A is ready, he begins by passing whatever club is in his right hand to Juggler B's left hand.

Then, continuing the cascade rhythm (do not change the alternating cascade movement of the hands!), Juggler A self-throws a club from his left hand to his right hand, passes the second time from his right hand to his partner's left hand,

pauses exactly one beat as if self-throwing again, and passes the third time from his right hand to his partner's left.

Make sure that the order of passes and self-throws occurs exactly as described.

The sequence for Juggler B is a little different. Juggler B catches the first incoming club in his left hand, waits until he is forced to empty the left hand in order to catch another incoming pass, and then self-throws from his left hand to his right hand. He catches the second incoming club in his left hand and the incoming self-throw in his right hand.

At this point Juggler B does nothing until there is a club in the air approaching his left hand. Before the incoming club arrives, Juggler B empties his left hand by self-throwing to his right hand and catches the third pass from Juggler A in his left hand.

Now, with a club in the air approaching his right hand, Juggler B empties his right hand by doing one of two things—either by self-throwing to his left hand and beginning a cascade pattern (this is the best choice at first, as it will give you time to stabilize your juggling pattern and prepare to pass) or by immediately passing back to Juggler A and repeating the entire sequence.

Whew! The description of events makes the

whole pattern seem far more difficult than it actually is. The most important thing to remember is that you must pass exactly in the order described. When passed clubs start arriving in your left hand, start a cascading rhythm. The rhythm will soon become automatic, and there will be little need for thinking, analyzing or remembering what needs to be done.

The cascade rhythm, with which you are intimately familiar, has a very regular beat (left hand toss, right hand toss, left hand toss, right hand toss, left hand toss). Continue that regular rhythm at a rate appropriate to the speed of the incoming passes until you are cascading three clubs.

Once you've practiced this pattern up to the point where neither partner has to cascade the 3c to regroup before passing them again, try passing the club that arrives in your right hand to your partner's left hand, not back to your own left hand.

Don't forget to run three around left-handed. Be patient. These are the building blocks of basic and advanced club-passing skills. Don't skimp on practice here. Impatience or lack of thoroughness will haunt you later on.

This pattern is very handy for advanced jugglers working on trick passes. While running this pattern you'll notice the moment when one juggler has already passed two clubs and has only one more club to pass. This last pass can now be thrown with full concentration. Similarly, it is an opportunity for the catcher to practice receiving the trick throw and integrating it into his or her cascade pattern. Try out your favorite trick throws. When you can throw every single club as a trick throw, and catch them too, you can feel confident that you will have little difficulty integrating that trick into a 2p6c (two people with six clubs) pattern.

Step Ten: Passing with Six Clubs

2p6c Patterns

Hey, what happened to 2p4c and 2p5c patterns? Logically they should fit in right here, but developmentally you're ready to go right to 2p6c, and that's what most people do.

Things get a bit more complicated as you add extra clubs to the juggling pattern, and the count and rhythm become extremely important. The count or beat denotes the rhythm of the pattern and indicates when to pass your clubs. The count of a particular pattern is determined by counting self-throws in the following way.

Call the first self-throw (the self-throw immediately following a pass) number one. Continue counting self-throws until a pass to another person has been thrown. That number, including the final pass, is the count of the pattern. Notice that passes are always thrown on the

highest number of the count. For instance, in a six-count pattern, the pass is always thrown after the fifth self-throw, or on the sixth beat.

Even-numbered counts indicate that passes will always be thrown with the same hand, either always with the right hand or always with the left hand. Odd-numbered counts indicate that both hands will be passing, one after the other, with some self-throws in between (except in a one-count pattern, which has no self-throws at all).

This nomenclature is the most comprehensive and also the most commonly used manner for discussing passing patterns today. It has superseded various other regional terminologies that needed constant clarification and has afforded cutting-edge passers a precise, common language with which to discuss what they are doing. Some advanced patterns can be incredibly difficult and complex. Describing patterns you

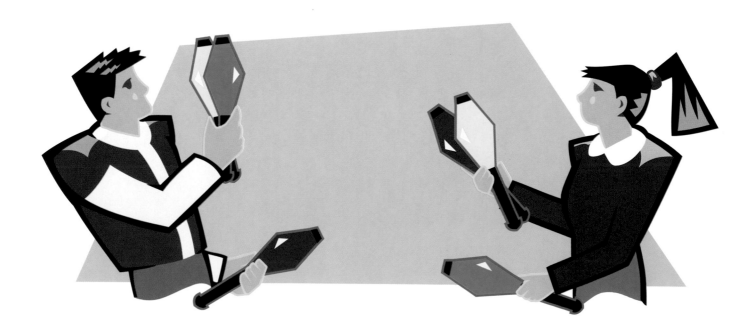

can barely conceptualize without a common language moves frustration to new and unnecessary heights.

Now, back to the pattern at hand.

To begin the 2p6c pattern, stand face-to-face with three clubs apiece—two clubs in your right hand and one club in your left hand.

Let's assume that you are going to pass with your right hand in a six-count pattern, the slowest and easiest standard passing rhythm.

How do we start? The most important thing about beginning, and a critical ingredient in the success of any pattern, is finding and maintaining a constant juggling speed. Both you and your partner must juggle at the same speed. In other words, your movements must be synchronized. Here's the standard way to get in sync.

With two clubs in your right hand and one club in your left hand, both you and your partner

should raise your right hands (some people like to raise both hands, but most of us are too lazy for that) and bring them back down to waist height simultaneously. This signals the beginning of the pattern.

Immediately start cascading your three clubs, beginning with a self-throw from your right hand. This is quickly followed by a self-throw from your left hand, a second self-throw from your right hand, and a second self-throw from your left hand, in that order.

The next natural self-throw becomes your first pass, and you begin the pattern proper. This is called a five-count start, or a slow start.

If you and your partner are not synchronized by the time your first pass is thrown—or even before—you should abort the pattern. Watch and listen to determine whether the pattern is in sync, and be aware of your partner's rhythm in

relation to your own. Don't bother continuing if you're not nearly perfectly in sync—it's just too frustrating. Give it up, regroup, and save your energies for a fresh start.

Eventually you will want to try a faster start. Begin together as above, with two clubs in your right hand and one club in your left hand. Raise your right hands and bring them back down again to signal the beginning of the pattern. Instead of cascading, however, throw your first club as the first pass of the pattern.

That's it. The fast start is simpler and faster than the five-count start, but it is also more difficult to perfect. The fast start gives you no opportunity to get in sync with your partner, and it requires you to be able to make an accurate pass directly out of a hand that's holding two clubs.

If this is too hard, practice holding two clubs in your right hand and passing them, one at a time, to your partner until it is comfortable.

You decide which start suits you.

Finally, we're ready to start the 2p6c pattern. Choose the start you like best and then begin (together, please).

On the first pass, both you and your partner toss the club in your right hand straight across to your partner's left hand. These passes occur simultaneously, are parallel passes with a single spin, and are executed in identical fashion (i.e., with the same speed, height, etc.). Keep cascading until the next sixth-count occurs and repeat the exchange of passes. Continue.

Strive to match the cascading rhythm of your partner. Inevitably there will be struggles, near disasters, and miracle recoveries that will alter your initial rhythm. Try to adjust, and you'll be able to keep it all in the air longer.

The only really new thing here is catching the pass and fitting it into your ongoing cascade. This, however, is very important. Work on it. You already know everything you need to know to succeed. Just practice until you can put everything you know into use.

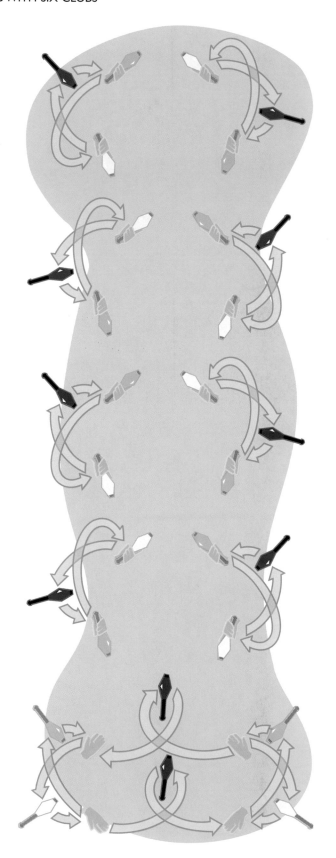

Even Counts

Learning to keep a 2p6c, right-handed, six-count pattern up in the air gives most jugglers a terrific sense of accomplishment. And it's well earned. Congratulations! Pat yourselves on the back and try the same thing using four-count rhythm.

The four-count rhythm works the same as the six-count rhythm, except that every other right-handed toss is passed instead of every third. The five-count start, however, never changes—it's always the same, giving you time to get in sync. This pattern is just a little quicker, and the passes occur more often. You know enough now to figure out the details. Try the four-count rhythm with your left hand as well.

Guess what's next? Right, the 2p6c, right-handed, two-count pattern. This pattern is even quicker, but you should be able to run it easily with some practice. Don't neglect the left-handed version, either. It will give your right wrists a rest and help avoid tendonitis.

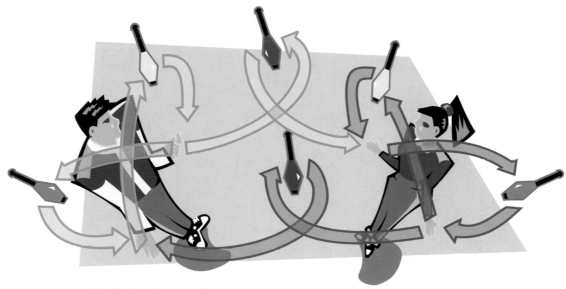

Left-Hand Even Counts

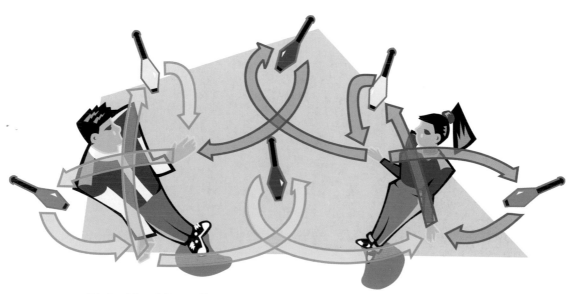

Right-Hand Even Counts

The 3-3-10

One would be hard-pressed to find a club-passing juggler who has not, as a novice, struggled with the 3-3-10. Technically the 3-3-10 is not a single pattern but a standardized sequence of even counts, originally popularized by Harry Lind. It consists of three six-counts, immediately followed by three four-counts, immediately followed by ten two-counts. The pattern can be run either right-handed or left-handed and is implicitly considered a rite of passage for passers.

After you and your partner have synchronized yourselves, exchange right-handed passes. Continuing your cascade, complete a left-handed self-throw, a right-handed self-throw, a left-handed self-throw, a right-handed self-throw, a left-handed self-throw, and then a right-handed pass to your partner. That's six counts in all. Repeat this pattern two more times.

That's three passes exchanged so far—the first "3" of the 3-3-10.

Proceed with a left-handed self-throw, a right-handed self-throw, a left-handed self-throw, and then a right-handed pass to your partner. This pattern is repeated two more times and accounts for the second "3" of the 3-3-10

The "10" indicates ten two-counts, also called shower passes. Proceed with a left-handed self-throw and a right-handed pass. The next nine consecutive right-handed tosses are passed to your partner, and the 3-3-10 is finally complete. Many jugglers end with a flourish, like a self-thrown triple caught in the left hand. It's up to you.

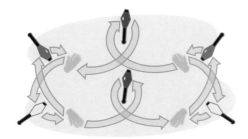

Start with a pass, then . . .

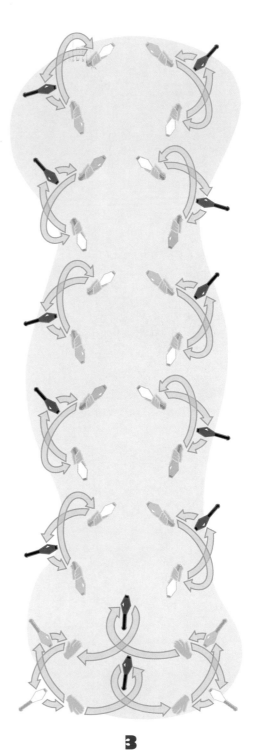

3

. . . repeat the right-handed, six-count pattern three times to complete the first "3" of the 3-3-10 . . .

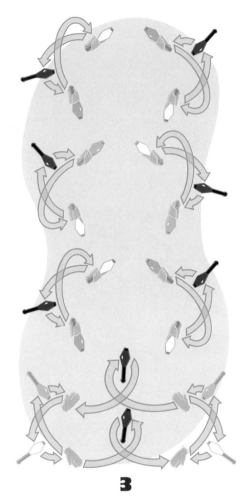

3

...repeat the right-handed, four-count pattern three times to complete the second "3"...

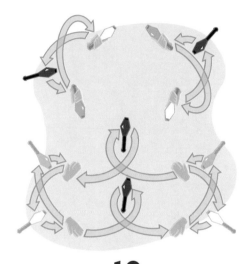

10

...and exchange ten right-handed passes to complete the sequence.

Odd Counts and The 4-4-8

In most odd-count patterns, every right-handed pass with your partner is followed, after the appropriate interval established by the count, by a left-handed pass. Likewise, every left-handed pass is followed, after the same interval of self-throws, by a right-handed pass.

The 4-4-8 is to odd counts what the 3-3-10 is to even counts. It is another traditional sequencing, consisting of four five-counts, immediately followed by four three-counts, immediately followed by eight one-counts. Here's how it works.

After your beginning, exchange right-handed passes with your partner.

Proceed with a left-handed self-throw, a right-handed self-throw, a left-handed self-throw, and another right-handed self-throw. Then, exchange left-handed passes with your partner. (Remember that five-count means you pass on every fifth beat, or after four self-throws.)

Follow the pass with a right-handed self-throw, a left-handed self-throw, a right-handed self-throw, another left-handed self-throw, and then a right-handed pass to your partner.

Next, make a left-handed self-throw, a right-handed self-throw, a left-handed self-throw, a right-handed self-throw, and then a left-handed pass to your partner.

Finally, finish the sequence

with a right-handed self-throw, a left-handed self-throw, a right-handed self-throw, another left-handed self-throw, and then a right-handed pass to your partner.

That makes four passes, and takes care of the first "4" in the 4-4-8.

To start the next sequence, immediately make a left-handed self-throw, a right-handed self-throw, and exchange left-handed passes with your partner. Follow this with a right-handed self-throw, a left-handed self-throw, and a right-handed pass to your partner.

Repeat this entire sequence once more.

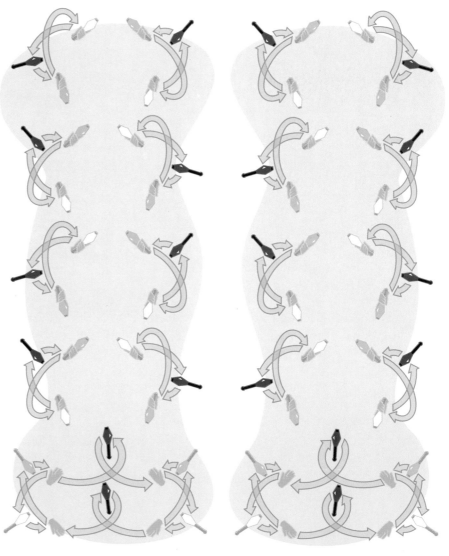

Start with a pass, then ...

Left-handed pass   **4**   **Right-handed pass**

... repeat the above ten-count pattern twice, passing alternately with your right and left hands for a total of four passes, to complete the first "4" in the 4-4-8 ...

STEP TEN: PASSING WITH SIX CLUBS

(In other words, repeat everything in the previous paragraph.)

That makes four more passes, and takes care of the second "4" of the 4-4-8.

Next, immediately pass with every hand for eight beats (four left-handed passes and four right-handed passes, alternately), beginning with a left-handed pass.

That's the "8" of the 4-4-8. Finish with the ending of your choice.

If you're still unknotting your eyeballs after those exhausting descriptions, relax. That's as bad as it gets, and there will be no test at the end of the book. If you understand the concepts, the rest will come in time.

Try breaking down the 4-4-8 (and also the 3-3-10) into smaller, more manageable chunks and practice each chunk individually until you are comfortable with the pattern. Afterward, you can link these chunks together. Once you're feeling comfortable with the sequences, try both the 3-3-10 and the 4-4-8 with double and triple throws.

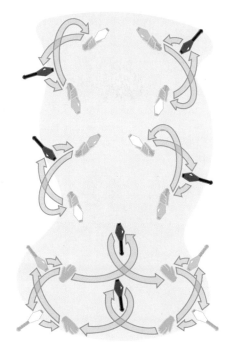

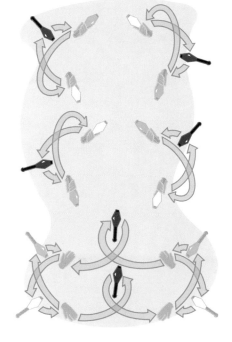

Left-handed pass **4** **Right-handed pass**

. . . repeat the above six-count pattern twice, passing alternately with your right and left hands for a total of four passes, to complete the second "4". . .

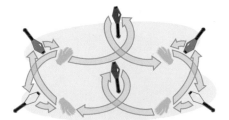

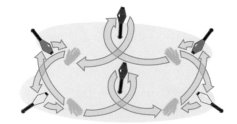

Left-handed pass **8** **Right-handed pass**

. . . and exchange right-handed and left-handed passes for a total of eight alternating passes to complete the pattern.

Two People, Six Clubs, and Your Imagination

The possibilities here are nearly endless. There are so many variations that it would take many volumes to describe them. I'll discuss a few variations that are frequently used to create interesting and beautiful patterns, and are helpful to know as ingredients in pattern-making.

Since there are three fundamental ways to run most patterns (right-handed, left-handed, and with an odd count), a complete investigation should explore all three. By describing patterns in a five-count rhythm, we hit three birds with one stone. Since the five-count is an odd count, it includes both right-handed and left-handed moves. As it is also relatively slow, we'll use it as the base count for the following.

Remember that in all counts the pass is always thrown on the last beat. That means that in the five-count, the club is passed on the fifth beat of the pattern. Since five is an odd number, the fifth position will alternate between the right hand and the left.

Notice that the fifth beat does not refer to either hand or to any one club throughout the pattern. What is being counted is the beat, the temporary position of the moving pattern.

Nevertheless, it is sometimes helpful to call the club that is being exchanged the #5 Club. Likewise, all clubs can be indicated by their numerical position in the count. Therefore, there will be a #1 Club, a #2 Club, a #3 Club, a #4 Club, and a #5 Club for each juggler in the pattern.

This naming convention makes it easier to

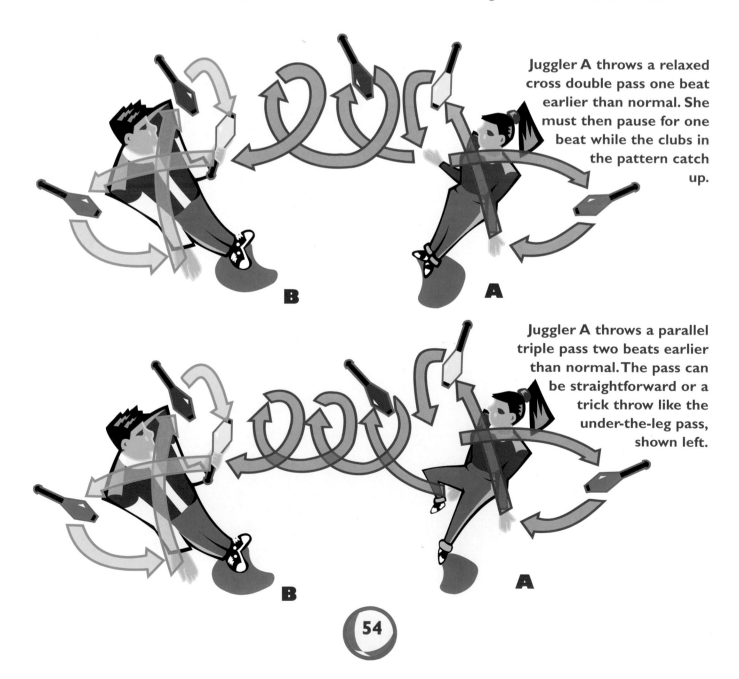

Juggler A throws a relaxed cross double pass one beat earlier than normal. She must then pause for one beat while the clubs in the pattern catch up.

Juggler A throws a parallel triple pass two beats earlier than normal. The pass can be straightforward or a trick throw like the under-the-leg pass, shown left.

describe many different passing patterns and variations, including early throws and kinks:

Just as it is necessary when passing a single to throw the club so that it enters your partner's pattern at the proper time, it is necessary to throw a double earlier than the single for it to arrive at the proper time. If you throw a relaxed cross double pass (be careful that your pass is not too quickly spun) with the #4 Club (i.e., one beat earlier than normal), the pattern continues smoothly. This #4 Club double pass takes the place of a #5 Club single pass.

Either or both partners may throw a double pass at any appropriate time. Try to become comfortable with these early throws, both for their intrinsic amusement value and as essential elements in advanced pattern juggling. Remember, the early double must be a cross pass in order to arrive in the same hand in which the singly spun #5 Club would have arrived. The opportunity arises in odd-count patterns to throw this early double alternately with both the right and left hands.

Notice that as Juggler A executes this early double variation with either hand, a one-beat pause is created during which she must wait for the clubs in the pattern to catch up. Juggler B, if he maintains a simple five-count, does not experience this pause in his juggle.

Similarly, early triples can be thrown with the #3 Club by either juggler. These triples must be thrown parallel, since they will skip two beats in the pattern and will be followed by a two-beat pause. Two beats is a lot of time, and you may want to fill it with gymnastics, dance moves, or other flourishes.

Quadruples with the #2 Club and quintuples with the #1 Club logically (but not so easily) follow. Feel free to try these early passes in any pattern you run, using any count.

None of these multiple-spin passes need be thrown in a straightforward way. They can be passed under the leg, behind the back (i.e., over the opposite shoulder), over the shoulder (i.e., over the same shoulder), overhand (also called chops), or whatever. Each trick throw has natural body movements that can be used to create harmonious effects, illusions, and even comedy.

When Juggler A throws an early triple, a two-beat pause appears in her pattern. You can fill this pause however you wish.

KINKS

This is an entertaining corollary to all this early throw stuff that has produced many pattern variations and can quickly turn a complicated but predictable two-person pattern into apparent chaos.

When you throw an early left-handed double to your partner's left hand, the club is essentially jumping ahead one position in the normal circulation of clubs through the hands. Specifically, that club is skipping your right hand.

It is also possible, however, for you to throw a club that skips *your partner's* left hand in the normal circulation of clubs. This is called a kink, because it causes a one-beat pause for the *receiver* in the pattern. If you cross throw a right-handed double to your partner's right hand instead of the parallel right-handed single to your partner's left hand that you would normally throw, that double will bypass your partner's left hand.

This may take quite a bit of practice to perfect. You've trained your left hand, your pass-catching hand, to always empty itself of clubs whenever a pass is expected. It's time to lose that habit! Once you and your partner get used to the kink pause and learn not to pre-guess which of your hands will be passed to, the kink will fit perfectly into the flow of the pattern.

Practice combining early throws and kinks for maximum mind-warping enjoyment. Singles and triples can also be thrown as kinks and (in an odd count) with either hand. Some combinations will work and some won't work within the confines of the count. Experiment with possible combinations to see what works best for you.

It's possible for all six clubs to be in the air at once if both jugglers throw a right-handed cross double, a left-handed cross double, and a right-handed parallel triple in unison on a right-handed two-count. Try it!

Step Eleven: Numbers Passing

In numbers patterns, there are more than three clubs being thrown per person. Everything boils down to technique. Once you've learned 2p7c (two people with seven clubs) and 2p8c (two people with eight clubs), you'll be able to add an extra club or two to any pattern.

Let's first look at 2p7c, the simplest numbers pattern possible. This pattern involves a new rhythm that's not often encountered in simple two-person situations but is basic to many numbers patterns.

With 2p6c, you're usually passing on the same beat as your partner. With 2p7c, however, this rarely happens. The pattern rhythm has to expand just a little to include that extra club. If it expanded a little further (to 2p8c), then both jugglers would be back to throwing at the same time.

Juggler A starts with two clubs in each hand, and Juggler B starts with two clubs in one hand and one club in the other. (Juggler A can also start with three clubs in one hand and one club in the other, but this is much harder. It takes quite a bit of practice to throw with any kind of accuracy from a hand with three clubs.) There is no easy way to start without jumping right in, so as soon as Juggler A (the juggler with four clubs always starts) begins to throw a pass, the pattern begins.

Juggler A's first move is to pass a right-handed double to Juggler B's left hand. She then self-throws a single from her left hand to her right hand. This pattern is then repeated. That's all Juggler A does throughout the pattern—pass parallel doubles every time a club is in her right hand and self-toss singles every time a club is in her left hand.

Juggler B waits until Juggler A's first pass is just about peaking on the way to his left hand, and then passes a double from his right hand to Juggler A's left hand. Juggler B then self-tosses a single from his left hand to his right hand, preparing to catch Juggler A's incoming pass in his now-empty left hand. That's it.

This will run a lot more smoothly if you take it easy, pass your doubles slowly at first, and keep the clubs away from your partner's face. It's easy to get so involved in the pattern that you ignore an incoming pass that's about to give you a fat lip.

When you are able, notice the rhythmical alteration of the passes as they take turns peaking

across the top. This will give you an immediate understanding of how your role and your partner's mesh, and how to constantly fine-tune the passes to keep them as perfectly out of sync as possible.

When you're ready for 2p8c, begin with two clubs in each hand. Start together and run it just like 2p6c. The only difference it that the pattern is much faster, and your passes and self-throws are thrown at almost exactly the same time. (Doubles are easiest.) After you get a lot of practice, you can fine-tune the rhythm of the pattern.

Armed with these basics of numbers passing, you're ready to add extra clubs to any pattern. You'll find lots of idiosyncrasies, but most patterns will readily adapt to the extra object.

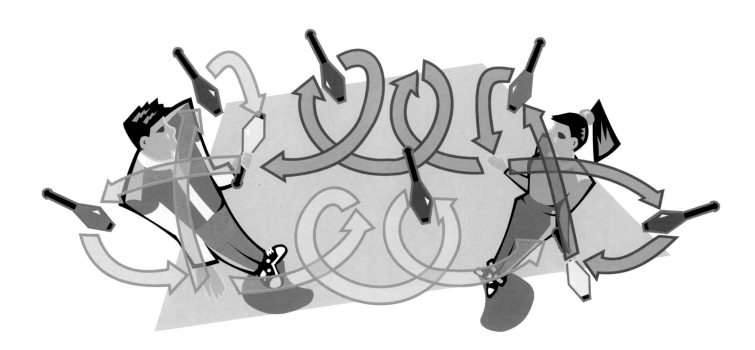

THE OLD CIGARETTE TRICK

The old cigarette trick is impressive to perform. A club flies soundlessly through the air and knocks a tiny cigarette out of an innocent volunteer's mouth. If the throw is just inches off the mark, the hapless volunteer is carried from the stage. In this litigious age, who would even dare?

By now you probably realize that the amount of control necessary to perform this trick is well within your grasp, if not already within your abilities. Still, this is a potentially dangerous trick, and certain precautions need to be taken before you attempt to knock a cigarette from the mouth of a complete stranger. Before you begin, here are a few helpful hints and precautions:

1. Experiment on a friend. He or she is less likely to deck you if you make a mistake. Also, you may want to have your volunteer wear a catcher's mask until you're sure that you won't hit his nose rather than the cigarette. This will allow you to relax and concentrate on positioning your throw. If your friend is a fellow juggler, be willing to take your turn as the cigarette holder and give him a try.

2. Use jumbo-sized cigarettes, big cigars, or even rolled-up newspapers until you get the feel of it.

3. Pick a slow count to start, like a six-count.

4. Don't try to hit the cigarette right off. Miss it by a few inches on the first couple of passes, and then work your way in as you become more proficient.

5. Try to find a volunteer who's close to your own height. The closer in height he or she is, the easier the trick will be to perform.

6. Don't use a lit cigarette. The ante goes up fast as they burn down, and you just don't need the pressure, believe me.

Step Twelve: Three-Person Patterns

Adding a third juggler greatly enlarges the patterning potential, automatically creating a third dimension and sequencing possibilities that are impossible with only two people. There are many configurations to choose from when a third person is added. Let's look at just a few.

The Feed

The feed is perhaps the most popular 3p (three-person) configuration. Here's how it works.

Two jugglers (called feedees) stand side by side facing a third juggler (called the Feeder).

All three jugglers begin together and stay synchronized throughout the pattern. That means that their right hands are always acting at the same time, and their left hands are always acting at the same time, though they may not always be performing the same action.

Let's call the juggler to the Feeder's right Feedee #1 and the juggler to the Feeder's left Feedee #2. On the first passing count, usually after a five-count start, the Feeder exchanges passes with Feedee #1. While this exchange

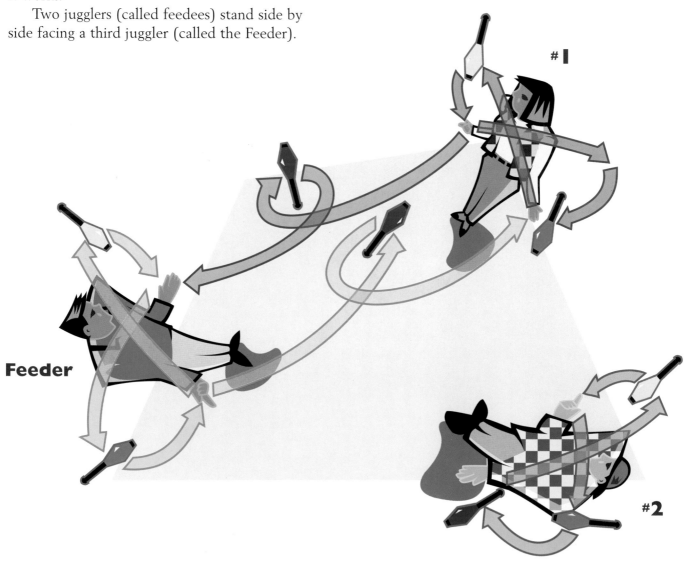

Feeder

#1

#2

is occurring, Feedee #2 is self-throwing. On the next passing count, the Feeder exchanges passes with Feedee #2, while Feedee #1 self-throws. Repeat. Try the feed with your left hand as well.

Due to the nature of the configuration, the odd counts create a special circumstance. When the Feeder is passing with both his right and left hands, one feedee must be passing only with his or her right hand, and the other feedee must be passing only with his or her left hand.

If Feedee #1 always passes with her right hand (most people think this is the easier

variation), the feed is called an outside feed, because the Feeder passes with his outside hand. If Feedee #2 is always passing with his right hand, the feed is called an inside feed. With an inside feed, there is more activity directly in front of the Feeder's face and more chance for collisions between clubs.

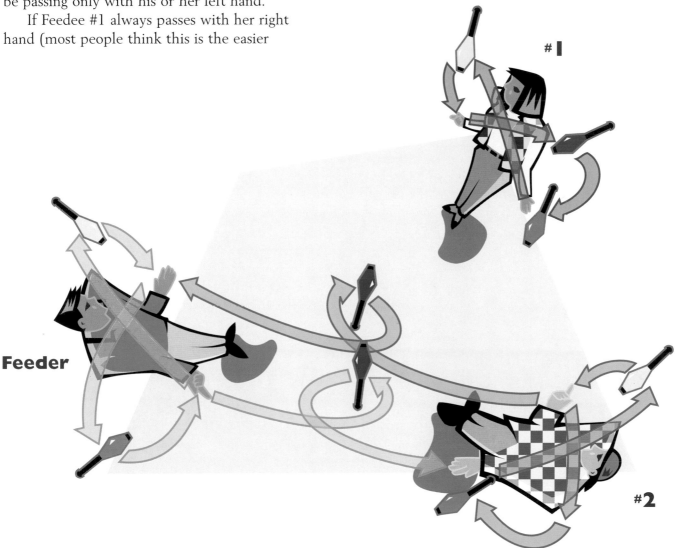

Three-Person Lines

Another very popular three-person config-uration is called a line. In the line, two jugglers (A and B) face each other, standing a little closer than they would in a two-person pattern. The third juggler (C) stands behind Juggler B, facing his or her back.

Many passing patterns are possible in this configuration. The most common—a 3p9c (three people with nine clubs), right-handed, six-count pattern—runs as follows.

Each juggler has two clubs in his right hand and one club in his left. They should begin with a slow five-count start. Juggler A is the leader of the pattern and the only juggler able to view the entire sequence. (Juggler C stands behind Juggler B and neither can see what the other is doing.)

He or she is therefore responsible for stopping the pattern if everyone is not in sync.

On the first and every passing count, Juggler A passes a single to Juggler B, Juggler B drops-back a double to Juggler C, and Juggler C passes (either a double or a long single) back to Juggler A. Often, Juggler C moves slightly to the right to be able to pass more easily to Juggler A. Juggler C should offer continual feedback to Juggler B about drop-back throws. Each person's rhythm will vary slightly due to variations in the length of passes, but try to keep the rhythm of the pattern fairly constant. Singles, doubles, or triples can be used to minimize rhythmic inequalities.

Don't forget to try left-handed passes as well as odd counts. Running any of these patterns backward will give Juggler C the chance to throw drop-ups to Juggler B.

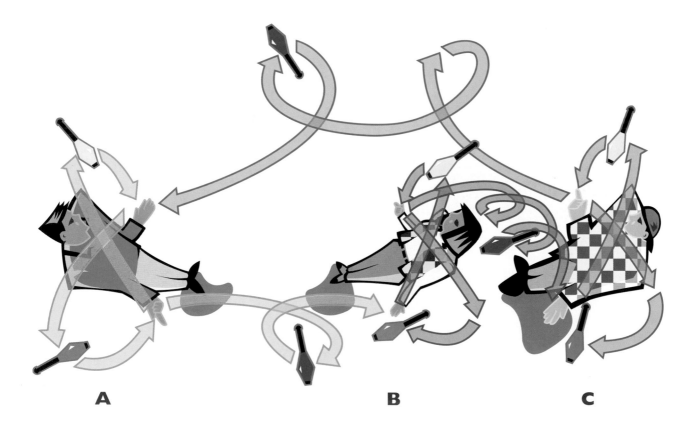

A   B   C

Triangles

The last common three-person configuration is the triangle. In this configuration, three jugglers stand in a triangle and space themselves so that each is equidistant from every other.

There are lots of possible patterns here, depending on who passes to whom and with which hand. Let's look at the easier ones.

If each person passes on an even count to the person standing closest to his passing hand, the result is called an outside triangle. If each person passes on an even count to the person standing farthest from his passing hand, the resulting pattern is called an inside triangle. Mastering the outside triangle requires good peripheral vision and short throws. Success with inside triangles, however, requires precise synchronization, since the three thrown clubs pass quite close to each other. Be gentle! Explosive collisions are not uncommon.

Don't forget the odd-count possibilities and all the potential variations with early and kink throws, doubles, triples, and tricks.

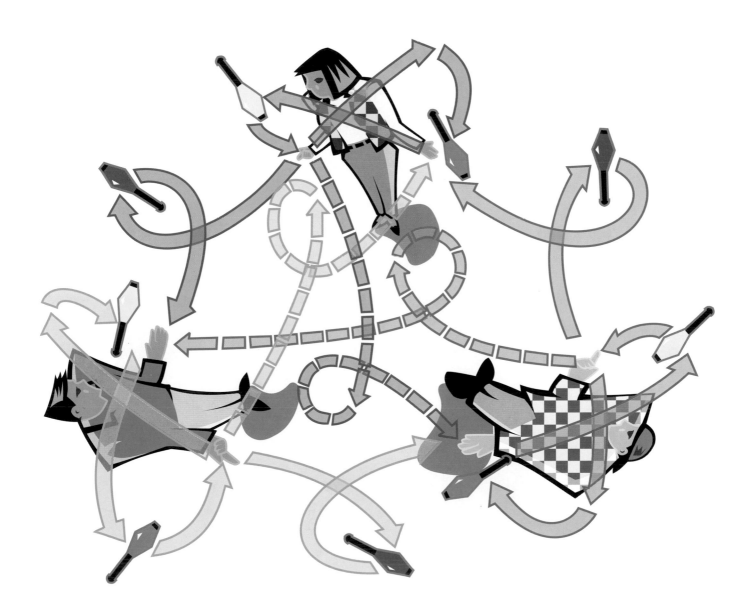

Step Thirteen: Passing with Four People

More jugglers make even more exotic configurations possible. However, using four jugglers often makes it necessary to run easier patterns, since success will often depend on the level of ability of the weakest link—the least competent juggler. Sometimes there are patterns with harder and easier roles in which a variety of levels of expertise can be accommodated. These patterns offer great opportunities for passers who want to work with more experienced jugglers.

In general, try to keep your patterns simple. Remember, the more jugglers you add to the configuration, the more clubs and people you need to coordinate.

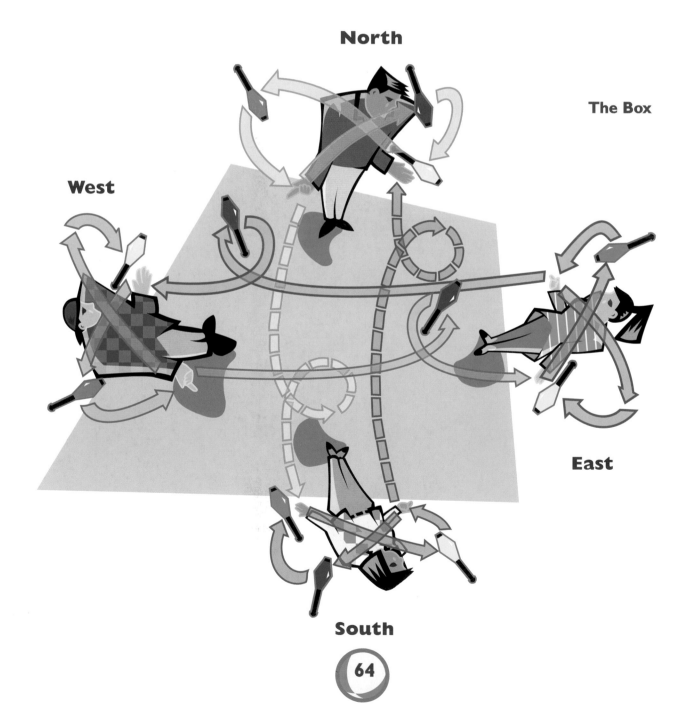

North

The Box

West

East

South

The Box

Arguably the easiest four-person configuration is the four-person box. Let's start with a 4p12c (four people with twelve clubs), right-handed pattern on an even count.

Four jugglers stand in a square, facing each other. Let's call them North, South, East, and West. Jugglers North and South exchange passes, as do jugglers East and West. All their right-handed tosses are synchronized, but when North and South are passing, East and West are self-throwing, and vice versa. This is all very straightforward. Now try it with your left hands.

When at least one pair can maintain a steady pattern of left-handed two-counts, let the other pair pass right-handed two-counts. The passes must be well synchronized, or you'll be picking up a lot of debris.

The most challenging variation of this pattern has both sets of partners passing on a one-count rhythm. Extreme precision and half-beat timing are both required to avoid collisions between clubs.

Without changing position, we can run another family of patterns called the square. In the square, each juggler passes to the person on his or her right and receives from the person on his or her left, or vice versa. This configuration is similar to the triangle and poses many of the same problems. The increased peripheral demands of the square, however, make this configuration even more difficult to master.

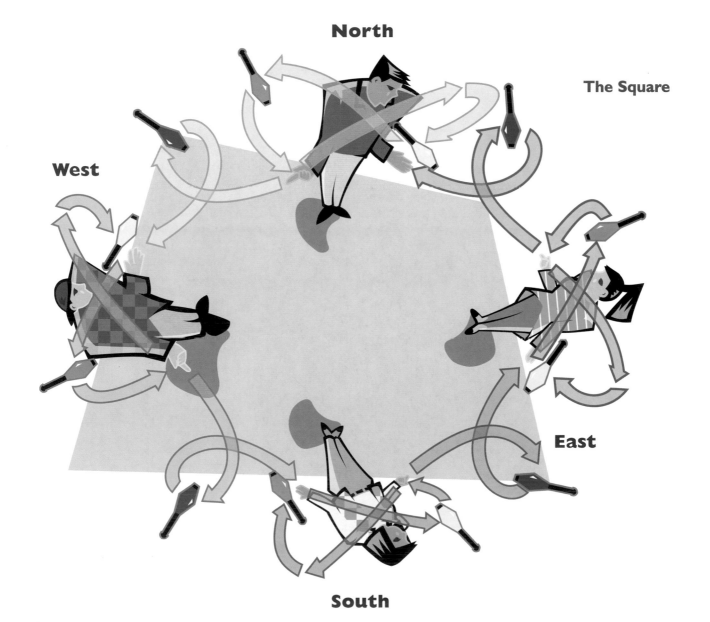

North

The Square

West

East

South

The Feed

You can add another feedee to the three-person-feed configuration for a variation on the standard feed.

Passing 4p12c on an even count, each juggler begins with two clubs in his right hand and one club in his left. The Feeder exchanges passes with Feedee #1 (the feedee on the far left end of the line) while the other feedees self-throw. On the next passing count, the Feeder exchanges with Feedee #2 (the feedee in the middle). Again, the other feedees self-throw. On the third passing count, the Feeder exchanges with Feedee #3 (the final feedee) while the other feedees self-throw.

When the next passing count comes along, the Feeder has two options: repeat the same order of passes or exchange passes with the feedees in reverse order. The first option is the least interesting, as it gives each feedee an equal and virtually interchangeable role.

In the second pattern, however, Feedee #2 passes twice as often as the other feedees. This option gives the four jugglers more variety and the opportunity to incorporate jugglers with different abilities into the pattern. There are three roles requiring three different levels of juggling prowess. Both Feedee #1 and Feedee #3 pass half as often as Feedee #2, and Feedee #2 passes half as often as the Feeder.

Passing 4p12c on an odd count is similar. If the Feeder passes to the feedees in the same order each time, then the feedees throw their passes on odd counts like the Feeder, just less often. If the Feeder reverses the order at the end of each cycle, Feedee #1 and Feedee #3 will pass with the same hand and Feedee #2 will throw twice as many passes with his or her alternate hand (e.g., if Feedee #1 and Feedee #3 are throwing with their right hands, Feedee #2 will throw with his or her left hand). Experiment for yourself.

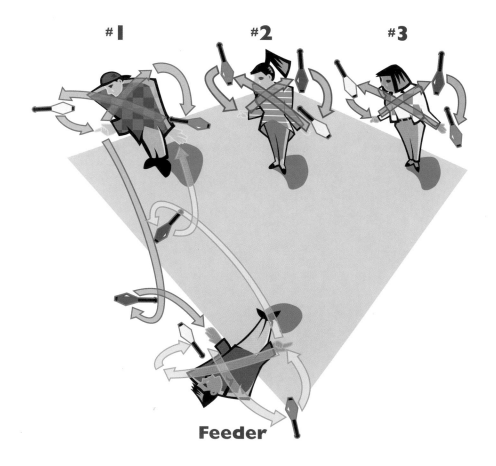

#1   #2   #3

Feeder

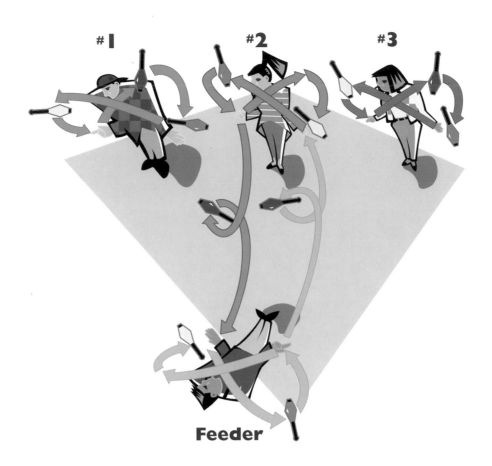

#1   #2   #3

Feeder

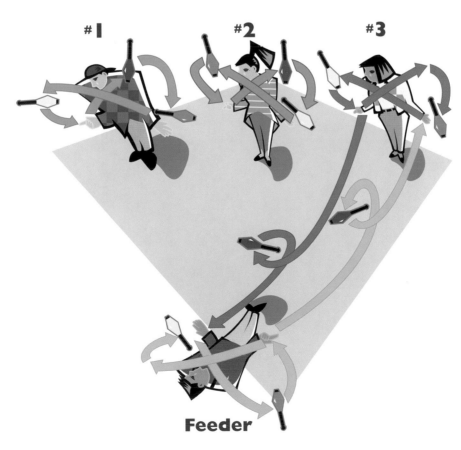

#1   #2   #3

Feeder

Other Props

Now that you've mastered the particulars of juggling, you may be looking for something new to toss about. Many juggling props suggest specific routines that were popularized by some of the most talented and creative performers in the juggling arena. Following is a list of props and some suggested uses. Please feel free to improvise and use these props in different ways. The best jugglers have always been those who created unique and innovative juggling routines.

SCARVES For small children and complete beginners, these relatively slow-moving objects help create a feel for the cascade at a manageable pace. Scarves are used much like balls and beanbags, and the routines employed are similar.

RINGS Rings are particularly good props for numbers jugglers. Thinner than balls, rings can be held more comfortably in your hand and can be thrown easily without colliding in midair. First introduced as an act by William Everhart around the turn of the century, large hoop rolling was popularized as a technical and artistic prop by Bob Bramson. Bramson was able to spin, balance, and juggle seven large wooden hoops at once.

BOXES Cigar boxes are a juggling prop that presents unique opportunities. Generally, one box is held in each hand and the third is sandwiched between them, untouched by either hand. The end boxes are switched from hand to hand while the third is left hanging in the air and re-caught once the switch is complete. Many variations exist in which the middle box switches positions with either end box, and boxes flip side to side, end over end, or travel around the body (under the leg, behind the back, etc.). Pirouettes are often performed while one, two, or three boxes are suspended in the air.

Kris Kremo, the best-known box juggler in the world, was the first to perform four pirouettes.

HATS Hat juggling is an entirely different style of juggling. Top hats and derbies are the standard tools, and the juggler works with a hat in each hand and one on the head. In a tradi-tional pattern, the juggler tosses a hat from his right hand to his left. The empty right hand then takes the hat from the head, leaving the head open for the hat currently in the left hand. Once this hat is placed on the head, the left hand is free to catch the tossed hat. These moves, when mastered, occur almost simultaneously, creating the illusion of a smooth flow of air. Variations in routines are greatly expanded when two hat jugglers work together. Many unique moves are possible in hat juggling, including hat balancing (on the brim), hat flourishes (twirls and flips performed by one hand with one hat), and various trick throws and catches (usually involving the foot or the head).

PING-PONG BALLS Ping-Pong balls are juggled with the mouth. The juggler moistens a ball and places it in his or her mouth. The head is then tipped back and the Ping-Pong ball is spit straight up into the air. The ball is then caught in the mouth and the process is repeated. A second Ping-Pong ball can be added to the mouth while the first is in the air. The juggler spits the second ball out in time to catch the first ball and con-tinue. Some jugglers add a third, a fourth, or even a fifth ball. Spaniard Gran Picaso, who developed this style of juggling, was the first to be able to juggle five Ping-Pong balls in his mouth.

DEVIL STICKS The devil stick routine originated in China and was introduced to the United States in the late 19th century. The equipment comprises three sticks, one in each hand (hit sticks, or handsticks) and one "devil stick" manipulated by the hit sticks. The devil stick is not touched unless it is grabbed and juggled club-like, or twirled like a baton.

Traditionally the devil stick is kept turning vertically in front of the juggler by means of precise hits near its ends to constantly reverse its direction of spin and to keep it from falling. The devil stick can also be kept rotating in the same direction around the tip of a hit stick, or it can be spun horizontally, like a helicopter blade, nudged now and then from below to keep it in the air. Good devil-stickers can manipulate separate devil sticks in each hand.

DIABOLO Asian children have been playing with diabolos for centuries. The diabolo is an egg-cup shaped cylinder, thinner in the middle than at the ends, that is rolled along a string tied at each end to sticks held in the hands. The toy works on a similar principle to that of the yo-yo. By moving the string across the center of the diabolo, the diabolo is spun faster and faster, developing gyroscopic stability. It can then be thrown and re-caught on the string (or another string) or passed around, over, and under parts of the body. Additionally, two and even three diabolos can be handled on the same string.

CUPS Juggling cups are the size and shape of cocktail shaker cups and are made of lightweight metal. One is held in each hand with one, two, or even three more cups nested inside. The juggler flips the nested cups in the air and catches them in another cup. The hand-held cups are often thrown and caught as well. Rudy Cardenas, a professional juggler, has worked with as many as ten cups at a time.

OTHER OBJECTS While it's not possible to name all the props that jugglers might use, chain saws and toilet plungers have both enjoyed sporadic and, fortunately, brief appeal. Knives (which are juggled) and swords (which are balanced) have also enjoyed sporadic popularity. You can juggle just about anything you can get your hands on. Experiment with juggling all kinds of objects and develop your own routine!

Types of Jugglers

The most memorable juggling performers have emphasized some aspect of juggling and performing above others. They have highlighted their strengths and have often expanded the known limits of their art by focusing their talents on highly specialized areas of juggling. The greatest jugglers have not tended to be the most versatile, but rather the most incredible.

What follows is an extremely brief overview of the more common areas of specialization and some of the most accomplished juggling performers.

STREET JUGGLERS Many jugglers begin on the street, where the stages are cheapest and most accessible. Street performers have been historically at odds with local businesses and the law and in constant competition with each other for the best venues. Regulation has tended to ease these problems, occasionally at the expense of spontaneity. Most acts eventually move off the street, a rare few having left their personal mark of excellence on a venue of notoriously haphazard quality.

In New York, Philippe Petit left his imprint on the street juggling scene in the 1970s. Well known for having tightrope-walked between the Trade Towers at the 110th floor, Petit entertained local audiences with his personal combination of juggling, rope-walking, and sleight of hand.

A veteran street performer and instructor, Laura Green (a.k.a. "Miss Tilly"), has also left her mark on the street juggling scene. Green's style and determination have inspired female jugglers throughout the United States. Her wacky and talented zaniness has also earned her a loyal following from Baltimore to Los Angeles.

skills, many of which he used during his extensive film career.

Bobby May, born in 1907 in Cleveland, Ohio, became one of the most famous American juggling performers. A comedy juggler, May realized early on that his audience wanted not only to be amazed, but to laugh. His effortless, energetic style was always accompanied by purely comedic moments that won him immediate respect and acclaim.

The Flying Karamazov Brothers, who are neither brothers nor Russian nor able to fly, have successfully mixed juggling, mime, high- and lowbrow comedy, and music for more than twenty years. Their routines are an entertaining brew of new vaudeville theater for everyman.

GENTLEMAN JUGGLERS Around 1890 the thriving European nightlife gave birth to a style of performing in which the formally attired juggler manipulated items from his immediate surroundings (usually a restaurant), including cups, plates, and hats. Gentleman jugglers are characterized by a leisurely elegance, and their routines are often thematically related. This was a popular variation on the standard performance of multiple unrelated tricks.

Dan Holzman, half of the comedy juggling team The Raspyni Brothers, is a well-known gentleman juggler performing today. Realizing early in his career that style was easier to sustain than world-class technical standards, Holzman created a successful routine as Danny Mulligan, the gentleman golfer/juggler.

COMEDY JUGGLERS The ability to make people laugh has always been better rewarded than the ability to juggle. While people enjoy watching creative and technically challenging routines, they love to laugh. Few jugglers, however, have been able to successfully combine comedy and technical prowess. There have been a few noted exceptions.

William Claude Dukenfield (better known as W. C. Fields) began his performing career in vaudeville as a tramp/juggler. Though now known as a movie star, Fields worked with the Ziegfeld Follies early in his career and never completely left behind his object-manipulation

AH, YES...

ARTISTIC JUGGLERS Though technique is an important ingredient in many performances, transcending it is the top priority for some jugglers. These jugglers tend to be some of the most creative and inventive juggling performers.

The originator of a unique style of contact juggling and the creator of the triangle (a juggling prop), Michael Moschen places more emphasis on discovery and originality than on any other aspect of juggling. While others spend years learning to juggle multiple objects, Moschen works to master one. One of the most creative jugglers working today, he has created whole routines in which he never releases or grabs an object.

Francis Brunn was the first to juggle both nine and ten rings, but he gave up this exhausting discipline to combine Flamenco dance with his juggling and acrobatic skills. Brunn went on to develop new precise and dramatic large-ball balancing and juggling techniques that became the hallmark of a long and classy career.

CLOWN AND CHARACTER JUGGLERS The fool or buffoon has always been a popular figure in human history. Watching someone who is even less competent than yourself and laughing freely at his failings can be immensely refreshing.

Claiming that it's more fun to watch a fallible person than a perfect one, Avner Eisenburg highlights everyman's weaknesses in his clown character's approach to juggling and the everyday world. Eisenburg, who played a lead role in the film *The Jewel of the Nile*, continues a tradition of vulnerable, endearing character performers that include Buster Keaton and Charlie Chaplin.

TECHNICAL JUGGLERS All juggling requires technique, but the term *technical juggler* has today come to refer to those whose performances rely heavily on their ability to execute routines of cutting-edge difficulty with a minimum of mistakes.

As of 1992, Anthony Gatto, a dedicated numbers juggler, could already juggle nine rings, nine balls, and eight clubs. At twenty-two he had already broken multiple world records and performed regularly for Las Vegas audiences for several years.

At the International Jugglers Association's annual festival in 1991, Sergei Ignatov flashed (i.e., threw and caught one complete cycle) eleven rings on his first attempt. At forty-one years old, this Soviet juggler, a product of a lifetime of disciplined circus-school training,

was considered by many to be the best juggler in the world. Dedicated to rigorous mastery of fundamentals often overlooked in the West, such as posture, balance, flexibility, and warmup, Ignatov juggled eleven rings as early as 1973. He was also the first to pirouette under seven rings.

Albert Lucas, also a multiple-record holder, is a specialist with rings and clubs. He is well known for performing juggling numbers while on ice skates, and performed for over a decade with the Ice Capades.

FEMALE JUGGLERS Despite the existence of expert female jugglers, women remain a minority in the juggling world. Some women, however, have made a significant mark and have led the way for other female performers.

Eva Vida's background was in ballet and art, but she became one of the best technical female jugglers of the 20th century. Able to juggle five clubs underneath either leg, Vida mastered many difficult numbers tricks with rings and developed an elegant parasol juggling routine.

Lottie Brunn belonged to a German-American juggling family that included her brother Francis, the first juggler to juggle both nine and ten rings. Despite her brother's prodigious talent, Brunn made a name for herself in the juggling arena as well. Long billed as "The World's Fastest Female Juggler," her talents were not limited to speed. At the age of fourteen, Brunn (much like her brother) was already juggling eight rings.

You and the Juggling World

If all has gone well, by the time you've reached this chapter you are an accomplished juggler. Congratulations!

Now what?

Meet others of your kind. There are people who teach themselves to juggle and spend years learning alone before they ever see another juggler. These people are delightful to watch—they tend to have unique, sometimes bizarre, styles. But they are a minority. Most jugglers learn with friends and gather often to work out and share ideas. Juggling clubs exist all over North America and in most countries around the world.

Today, the largest juggling club in the world is the International Jugglers Association (IJA), headquartered in Montague, Massachusetts. Founded in 1947, it's a nonprofit organization dedicated to the education and service of jugglers and juggling worldwide. At present, the IJA facilitates communication between 4,000 members in more than fifty countries around the world, publishes a monthly magazine called *Juggler's World*, hosts two annual festivals, serves as an umbrella group assisting more than sixty affiliates around the continent, and works to record and maintain the history of juggling.

For information about the IJA, write to:
P.O. Box 218
Montague, MA 01351
phone: (413) 367-2401
fax: (413) 367-0259
email: ijugglersa@aol.com

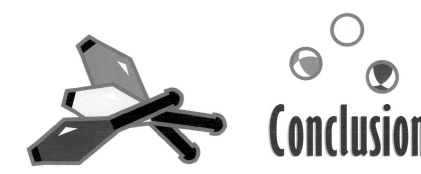

Conclusion

Most non-jugglers will tell you that juggling is throwing stuff into the air and catching it again. That's certainly not wrong. But you might as well say that painting is drawing in color, or that ballet is jumping around to music.

Juggling can be a portable job and can take you around the world. It can lead you into theaters, circuses, schools, movies, or nowadays even political office. It can provide a good workout, for juggling is both athletics and art, solitary or social or spiritual, or something unknown, waiting for you to invent.

Juggling is an expression of *you* through the manipulation of objects. There are no limits to what you can do when you juggle—only what you want to do. Your discipline has earned you mastery of the basics of juggling.

Enjoy them! What you do with them is who you are.

Glossary

Antipodism   A style of foot juggling common in theater shows and circuses in which the performer lies on his back with his legs toward the ceiling and manipulates, spins, rolls, tosses, and catches objects on the soles of his feet.

Back-to-front   A passing configuration for two people in which one juggler stands behind the other, facing his back.

Beat   *See* Count

Bounce juggling   A form of juggling in which balls are bounced off the floor and caught as they bounce back up. The balls can be tossed gently so that they bounce in small arcs up to your hand or be thrown (forced bounce) at the floor and caught on the rebound.

Cascade   A standard and fundamental juggling pattern in which props travel through the hands in a sideways, figure-eight pattern.

Club   The juggling prop shaped like a bowling pin or bottle. Clubs are usually made of lightweight, sturdy plastics and come in a variety of colors.

Club swinging   A style of juggling in which two clubs are manipulated, one in each hand, without letting go of either club. Also known as Indian club swinging.

Configuration   The position in which the jugglers stand in relation to one another while performing a routine.

Contact juggling   A style of juggling in which the juggled or manipulated object is moved in continuous contact with the juggler's body—on, around, over, and under.

Count   The underlying rhythm of a passing pattern. Also known as a beat.

Cross pass   A pass in which the juggled prop crosses an imaginary line between two jugglers.

Devil stick   A stick of Chinese origin that is usually kept turning vertically in front of the juggler by means of precise hits near its ends to constantly reverse its direction of spin and to keep it from falling. When juggled expertly, the stick appears to be suspended in the air.

Diabolo   A prop of Chinese origin consisting of an egg-cup shaped cylinder—thinner in the middle than at the ends—that is rolled along a string tied at each end to sticks held in the hands. By whipping the string from side to side, the diabolo is spun very rapidly and can be rolled, tossed, and caught on the string.

Doubles   A toss in which a prop rotates twice before it is caught.

Drop-back   A move in a passing pattern in which you throw a prop over your head or shoulder to a partner who is standing behind you.

Drop-up   A move in a passing pattern in which you throw a prop to a partner who is standing with his back toward you. Drop-ups and drop-backs are used when jugglers are standing in a back-to-front configuration.

Early throw   A move in a passing pattern in which a prop is thrown earlier than expected, creating a pause in the thrower's juggling pattern.

Exchange   The term used to describe the standard two-ball juggling pattern. It is also used to describe simultaneous passes between juggling partners.

Fast start   The beginning of a passing pattern in which the first thrown club is passed to your partner.

Five-count start   The beginning of a passing pattern in which the first four throws are self-throws and the fifth throw is a pass to your partner. This start gives the jugglers in the passing pattern time to get in sync before beginning the passing pattern proper. Also known as a slow start.

Flash   In attempts to juggle large numbers of objects, a flash is a successful juggle of at least one separate throw and one separate catch of each object before dropping.

Forced bounce   The movement in a bounce juggling pattern in which the prop is thrown downward and caught on the rebound.

Four-four-eight (4-4-8)   A traditional and standardized sequence of throws consisting of four five-count passes followed by four three-count passes followed by eight one-count passes.

Half-shower   The movement in which the props juggled by one hand follow a cascade pattern while those in the other hand follow a reverse-cascade.

Handle   The long, narrow part of a club by which it is thrown and caught.

Indian club swinging   *See* Club swinging

Kick-up   The term used to describe the use of the feet to toss a juggling prop up to the hand.

Kink   A move in a passing pattern in which a prop is thrown so that it arrives in the hand opposite from which the receiver is expecting it (e.g., the right hand instead of the left hand), creating a pause in the receiver's juggling pattern.

Multiplexing   A style of juggling in which more than one prop is thrown with each throw, enabling the juggler to keep more props in the air with fewer throws and catches.

Parallel pass   A pass in which the juggled object does not cross an imaginary line between two jugglers.

Passing   The exchange of props between two or more jugglers.

Pattern   The path that the juggled object travels as it moves through the hands.

Pause   The moment when movement is temporarily halted by variations in the catching or throwing of a prop. Pauses, for example, occur when early passes, kink passes, and many other trick throws and catches are performed.

Pirouette   A 360-degree turn executed by a juggler during a movement.

Reverse-cascade   The same basic pattern as the cascade, but in reverse. In the cascade each ball is thrown under the incoming ball, while in the reverse cascade each ball is thrown over the incoming ball.

Self-throw   A toss from one juggler's hand to the other. Also known as a self-pass.

Shower   A fundamental juggling pattern in which the props move in one large circle rather than in the "lazy eight" pattern of the cascade.

Shower passing   A rhythm for continuous passing in which every other throw is passed to your partner (i.e., if you begin passing with your right hand, every throw from your right hand will be passed, and every throw from your left hand will be self-thrown). Also known as two-count passing.

Single   A toss in which a prop completes slightly more than one revolution (about $1\frac{1}{4}$) before it is caught.

Slow start   *See* Five-count start

Start   The term used to describe the beginning of a routine or the resumption of a routine after a pause.

Three-three-ten (3-3-10)   A traditional and standardized sequence of throws consisting of three six-count passes followed by three four-count passes followed by ten two-count passes.

Two-count passing   *See* Shower passing

About the Author

Richard Dingman is the author of *Patterns*, a technical book about juggling passing patterns, and *The Little Book of Juggling*. He is secretary and treasurer for the International Jugglers Association (IJA), and works as an adventure education instructor. He has street-juggled throughout Europe and North America, and has judged several international juggling competitions. He lives in Montague, Massachusetts, with his girlfriend, Ginny Rose, and their dog, Astro. He dedicates this book to his parents, for whom no amount of thanks is too much.